Pat Maier

Liz Barnett

Adam Warren

David Brunner

Using Technology in Teaching & Learning

KOGAN
PAGE

 Interactive Learning Centre

First published in 1996 by the Interactive Learning Centre, University of Southampton
This edition published in 1998

Kogan Page Limited
120 Pentonville Road
London N1 9JN
and
22883 Quicksilver Drive
Stirling, VA 20166, USA

British Library Cataloguing in Publication Data
A CIP record for this book is available from the British Library.
ISBN 0 7494 2516 4

Typeset by Kogan Page
Printed and bound in Great Britain byBiddles Ltd, Guilford and King's Lynn

Contents

4   *Using computers to communicate with and between students*

Preface

The book was originally funded by HEFCE, SHEFCE, HEFCW and DENI under the Teaching and Learning Technology Programme (TLTP) and published within the TLTP programme as *Technology in Teaching and Learning: a guide for academics.*

The Teaching and Learning Technology programme (Phase 1 and 2) was a large national programme from 1992–1996, with an estimated outlay of £44 million. This period focused on teaching innovation using current learning technologies, with project consortia from UK universities producing computer-aided learning packages. A promotional CD-ROM of some of the packages produced can be obtained from: TLTP, Northavon House, Coldharbour Lane, Bristol, BS16 1QD, England.

In addition to the production of material, a group of eight universities were institutionally funded to work at an infrastructural level to move the culture of their university towards an increased use of learning technologies. The Interactive Learning Centre at the University of Southampton was set up under this institutional phase of the programme.

The guide was originally conceived and designed by Dr Haydn Mathias and myself as a reflection of the learning technology staff workshops held at the Interactive Learning Centre (ILC) of the University of Southampton. The guide comprised two books: one on the application of technology to teaching and learning and the other as a technical resource on understanding the technology. The books were accompanied by a video giving an overview of the technologies and their use.

I would like to thank Leslie Mapp from the Open Learning Foundation for his constructive advice during the early stages of the design. I would also like to thank our reviewers, Dr David McConnell from the University of Sheffield and Dr Chris Colbourn from the University of Southampton, who dissected the draft and gave us good advice leading to the final product.

The video of case studies was produced by Peter Phillips from the University of Southampton. We are also very grateful to those who gave us their time and agreed to appear in the video: Dr Chris Colbourn (University of Southampton), Dr Christine Steeples (University of Lancaster), Malcolm Ryan (University of Greenwich), Dr David Fincham (University of Keele) and Dr Philippa Reed (University of Southampton).

Thanks also go out to our technical team on the original guide: for graphic design and page layout, Neil Dawes, Catherine Poupart and Claire Ausden from Teaching Support and Media Services at the University of Southampton.

We also extend our thanks to our editor, Margaret Shaw, who painstakingly went through our manuscript with a fine-tooth comb, weeding out inconsistencies and clumsy expressions.

This commercial publication of the guide is sold as two separate books: *Using Technology in Teaching and Learning* and *Technology in Teaching and Learning: An Introductory Guide for academics*. We have had very positive feedback from users of the guide. The 'Using' book looks at the application of learning and technology while the 'Introductory' book is a reference to understanding the technology. The 15 minute video (available from Southampton University) is ideal as a training tool as it gives a quick overview of learning technologies. Feedback from those using the guide to date have said they use the 'Using' book and video as part of training material for staff, while the 'Introductory' book has been used as a back-up resource for trainers and by other staff on student teaching programmes.

Pat Maier
Educational Developer
Interactive Learning Centre
University of Southampton

Permissions

I would like to acknowledge the permissions given to use the following illustrations; listed in the order they are presented in the book.

Section 2.4.3 Web screen from:TML: Tutorial Mark-up Language
Kind permission for reproduction granted by the Institute for Learning and Research at the University of Bristol, UK.

Section 3.4.1 Case Study 3, Web screen from: Sci-Journal
Kind permission for reproduction granted from Patrick Fullick, Education Department, University of Southampton, UK.

Section 3.4.1 Case Study 4, Web screen Thinking and Knowing,
Kind permission for reproduction from Professor Stevan Harnard,Psychology Department, University of Southampton, UK.

Section 3.4.1 Case Study 5, Web screen from DIY Glycolysis Home Page
Kind permission from Jon Maber from the Bionet Teaching and Learning Technology Programme at the University of Leeds, UK.

Section3.5.1 Figure 3.11 Select a Document screen from Microcosm
Kind permission for reproduction from Multicosm, UK.

Section 3.5.1 Figure 3.12 Course modules in Economics and Figure 3.13 Stile 'Buttons'
Kind permission of Simon Fitzpatrick at the University of Leicester, UK.

ICONS

pencil: activity section

open book: references to other material

cross: cross references to material further in the book or its partner book

exclamation mark: please note

Foreword

The inclusion of learning technologies within education at all levels is becoming a reality; it is something institutions, departments and individual members of staff cannot ignore. Learning technologies have opened up a world of multimedia resources that can be quickly searched and flexibly accessed across computer networks, not only locally but also worldwide. In addition, they can be combined within the rapidly growing world of communications via email, conferencing systems and the World Wide Web.

The infrastructure for these 'new' worlds is already being established in many areas of society, and we shall see an explosion of their use within the next five years. As providers and users of these technologies, educators and students need an understanding of how they can enhance the university programme. This will inevitably lead to new methods of teaching and learning, and to an exciting debate on the educational implications of technology.

This book looks at the issues involved in integrating these learning technologies within teaching and learning, while setting the issues involved in a wider educational context.

Cross references are made within this book to a further book, *Technology in Teaching & Learning*, which provides the basic knowledge for getting started with the technology.

Wendy Hall
Professor of Electronics and Computer Science
University of Southampton

Dr Haydn Mathias
Director
Teaching Support and Media Services
University of Southampton

1 Educational perspectives

1.1 *Why change how we teach in higher education?*

This resource learning pack is all about innovation and change in teaching and learning in higher education. Its focus is on the roles of information technology and computer technology in improving the quality of teaching and learning, and on looking to future possibilities and challenges.

But why bother? Why change?

For most of us, there are likely to be two primary motivations – or types of pressure – to change:

- external – changes in who we teach, what we teach, what resources are available to us for teaching, and how our teaching is judged by others; developments in educational research, which highlight alternative approaches to teaching and learning

- internal – personal interest in improving and developing our teaching, based on current experience.

If your motivation for picking up this package is primarily personal – perhaps you are facing a particular teaching problem, and are looking for ways to solve it – it may be worth going directly to the sections on teaching and learning. You can always come back to this section later!

If you have a more general interest in exploring why and how you might change the way you are teaching now, it will be worth spending some more time on considering the effects that external pressures are having on you. Different pressures will suggest different options for change. The following pages look at some of these pressures, which you will find grouped into four key categories:

- pressure from changes in the students we teach
- pressure from new public expectations of higher education
- pressure from the impact of technology on the production and dissemination of knowledge itself
- developments in educational research which suggest more effective and efficient approaches to teaching and learning.

1.1.1 Changes in the students we teach

The first and most obvious change is in the nature of the student body itself.

- Student intake has more than doubled since 1982 – and this has not been matched by a commensurate increase in numbers of lecturers, nor in resources for support of teaching.

- Entry qualifications have changed, with more students entering on the basis of 'non-traditional' qualifications.

- Mature student intake has risen considerably. For example in the United States between 1980–1990, student enrolment for those under 25 years increased by 3%, compared to a 34% increase in enrolments for students over 25 years.[1]

- There are more overseas students, both from Europe and from further afield.

- There are more part-time students, often faced with both family and employment pressures on top of their degree work.

As a university lecturer today, you are likely to be facing much larger and more diverse classes than you would have done ten – or even five – years ago. Yet much of university education is still geared to the lecture/seminar/tutorial (and sometimes laboratory/practical) system. It is heavily dependent on the face-to-face contact between lecturer and student which you yourself probably experienced. There is ample evidence to indicate that on the whole, teachers are prone to replicate the teaching they have experienced – unless they actively pursue development in this field. The difficulty with trying to continue today what has been done in the past is that it will inevitably put an ever-growing strain on you as you try to provide adequate support to students. Furthermore, given the current student body, this system may simply not work as well as it used to.

Figure 1.1 highlights some of the pressures created by increased numbers and diversity. You will find several of these issues picked up again later in the teaching and learning sections.

J.M. Consulting, HEFCE Publication (1997)[1]

Figure 1.1

Problems for lecturers created by increasing student numbers and student diversity	Sections from Teaching and Learning which address these problems
Classes outgrow lecture theatres	2.2/2.3
Student access to library resources becomes more difficult	3.1/3.2
Seminar groups get bigger so there is less opportunity for active discussion between students	4
Seminar-based courses have to be turned into lecture-based courses, as groups get too big for effective seminars	2.2
Academic staff have too many personal tutees to give them the one-to-one attention they need	4.1/4.4/4.5
Having to spend more time on assessing large groups reduces the quality/efficiency of feedback to students	2.4
Having students joining courses with different 'entry levels' creates a need for more specialist support for different types of student and for greater flexibility in courses	3.2/3.4/3.5
Some students have to fit their studies into existing work and family commitments	3.4/4.6
As part of their studies, mature students expect or need to build on their past work and life experience	3.4

There are further important, but less obvious, changes in students. First, an increasing proportion are contributing much more of their own money towards their education – leading to an increasing 'consumer orientation' within higher education. This adds two new pressures:

- Increasing questioning by students of what they are 'getting for their money' – raising the importance of taking on board student feedback about courses and addressing student concerns.

- Greater expectation from students that their higher education will somehow improve their employment prospects, and will start to provide them with some of the skills they need for work – making it more important for universities to consider the extent to which degree courses should and can be seen as preparation for employment.

Secondly, many students are entering higher education with a different level of awareness about IT and computers than we, their predecessors, did. They (and their future employers) increasingly expect not only access to new technology, but also experience in developing their skills in its use.

To put this point into context, look at Activity 1A on page 6. In the first column are a range of possible IT skills we might expect students to develop. Looking back, five years ago we probably wouldn't have *expected* any of them. But what of today? Look down the list and tick those you would expect of your current students. Then look at the next column to assess for yourself whether the courses in your department do anything to help students develop these skills. Finally, are there adequate facilities to enable students to practise their IT skills?

Personal experience with computers and research both demonstrate that IT competence can be achieved only through regular, frequent use of IT. If students need these skills in the future, and have already started to develop them prior to entering university, it is the duty of university teachers to strengthen and develop these skills. This does not simply mean telling students that essays must be word processed: it involves providing tuition on IT skills, getting students to apply those skills in a variety of ways, and finding ways of assessing them. This pressurises us to change what and how we teach, for core IT skills need to be embedded in the curriculum.

This book is not specifically designed to help students to develop IT skills. However, many of the ideas in the other sections will contribute to this.

Activity 1A **Your expectations of student IT skills**

Student IT skills/expectations	What I expect of students	Do I prepare students to develop these skills?	Are there ample facilities to enable students to skills they've developed?
Students with some IT skills (eg word processing) on entry			
Students with a range of IT skills by graduation	(List the skills you expect to be developed for each of the degree programmes you are involved in)	(Tick those you actively help students to develop)	
Students able to use some form of computer-based bibliographic search facility by final year			
Students using internal email systems			
Students starting to use the WWW/Internet			

Feedback

Clearly, if you have a mismatch between items you ticked in the second column and those you ticked in the final two columns, there is a mismatch between the expectations you have of your students and the support they get from you. This suggests a need for change!

1.1.2   *Public and political expectations of higher education*

Beyond students, there is a wider public with an important stake in higher education. This includes:

- public and private sector employers of graduate students
- the bodies funding higher education (especially the HEFCE)
- central government
- the tax payer
- the individual sponsors of students (parents, students themselves, employers etc).

These groups are increasingly demanding that higher education accounts for the public funds it gets. They also expect higher education to pay greater attention to the relevance of student degree programmes to their future employment prospects.

Public accountability in higher education

The most obvious manifestation of the 'accountability' pressure is the Assessment of the Quality of Education exercise (QA) of the UK Higher Education Funding Councils (HEFC). The assessment has two components: a written document and an assessment visit.

If you work in the UK and your department has already experienced QA, you may already be familiar with the kinds of issues on which both the written document and the visits focus. If not, here is a flavour of what is required. The assessment process calls first for a clear articulation of:

- **Aims**
  What abilities and attitudes can potential 'stakeholders' – such as academics, students themselves, employers and sponsors – expect of students who have been successful?

- **Objectives**
  What is a 'successful' student? What are the intended learning outcomes? These might consist of acquisition of knowledge, development of understanding, development of skills and abilities (including generic or transferable skills), development of attitudes towards learning, etc.

- **Student learning resources**
  What resources are available to achieve these objectives? This calls for factual descriptions of the student profile, the staff profile, and the learning resources deployed by the institution to support the subject being assessed.

This is then used as the context against which departments evaluate the quality of education provided, in terms of the six profile areas outlined in Figure 1.2 below.

Figure 1.2   HEFCE's Quality Assessment Profile Areas (UK)

Curriculum design, content	Looking for a clear content and structure to courses in a given subject area, with articulation of intended outcomes of teaching and learning, and indication of the opportunity for progression to postgraduate study and employment, through personal development and the development of subject skills, transferable skills
Teaching, learning and assessment	Looking for a coherent strategy which implements the curriculum through appropriate methods of teaching and assessment; again, emphasis given to the development of subject-specific knowledge, understanding and skills as well as to generic/transferable skills
Student progression and achievement	Looking for outcomes of assessment during and at the end of a course of study
Student support and guidance	Looking for evidence of an overall strategy for student support, along with specific structures (eg induction, personal tutoring, remedial work, pastoral care, careers support)
Learning resources	Looking for an overall strategy for learning resources, along with specific provision (including library, IT, teaching facilities and technical support)
Quality assurance and enhancement	Looking for evidence of quality audit features (eg curriculum/ course review, staff development, appraisal of teaching, how the final degree outcomes compare with similar in the field, and what impact the quality audit process has on student experience)

As you can see from Figure 1.2 considerable reference is made to student employment, and the extent to which the student's learning experience is likely to have direct and indirect future benefits. Brief reference is also made to IT. The concern here is not simply with the level of hardware and software provision in the institution, but also with how this is integrated into teaching and learning.

Now review the major areas considered in Quality Assessment in Activity 1B below, and use it to explore the educational experience provided by you and your department. Identify those areas you think may need to be strengthened in order to meet the HEFCE QA criteria.

Activity 1B Facing up to Quality Assessment criteria

QA areas of assessment	Tick if satisfactory and note any areas where you or your department may be weak
1 Clear expression of the educational aims of the department written down	
2 Course objectives described in terms of learning outcomes relevant both to your academic discipline, and to the potential needs/interests/concerns of your students, their sponsors and their future employers	
3 Clarity/coherence/structure of curriculum	
4 Objectives appropriately matched to teaching and assessment methods (with an eye to both subject-specific and generic or transferable skills and abilities)	
5 Awareness of how students progress through their courses, and of how your courses compare with others of a similar nature elsewhere	
6 Provision of adequate pastoral and academic support for students	
7 Learning resources sufficient to support the teaching/learning process	
8 Ways in which you can demonstrate that quality is 'assured'	

Feedback

If you have been unable to tick any of the points indicated above, this suggests a need to do some work on course development in your department. This pack does not aim to address all these issues – but many of the ideas in it will help. In particular, it should prove useful in helping you to think through item 4 (how you match objectives with teaching and assessment methods) and item 7 (the learning resources needed to support given approaches to teaching and assessment).

The Assessment of the Quality of Education in the UK is relatively new, unpopular with most academics, and likely to evolve and change over time. However, it is unlikely to go away in the foreseeable future, and more likely to change in the assessment mechanisms than in the broad areas with which it is concerned. It is also highly likely that before long the outcome of assessment will in part determine the financial resources allocated to a university or university department. This makes the accountability process both 'stick and carrot' as a motivator for change (for the better, we hope) in higher education.

HEFCE Quality Assessment Reports
http://www.niss.ac.uk/education/hefce/qar/

In the United States there is no exact sister organization to the funding councils in the UK. Every state is responsible for its own higher education system. In the United States there are some 2,200 classified higher education institutions, although private institutions outnumber public ones. There is no standard accreditation system across the United States, thus making it somewhat difficult to assess student outputs across higher education institutions.[1]

In Australia, the sister organization to the Higher Education Funding Council for England, is the Higher Education Council. The university system here (comprising 38 Universities in total) is seen to be of high quality. The Graduate Careers Council of Australia contributes to this together with the Committee for Quality Assurance in Higher Education.[1]

The International Network for Quality in Higher Education was established at an international conference held in Hong Kong 1991. It is a network of worldwide members that collects and disseminates information on assessment and the maintenance of quality in higher education. It also has a list of quality assurance agencies in a variety of countries.

Higher Education Council (Australia)
http://www.deet.gov.au/nbeet/hec/hec.htm

Australian Vice-Chancellors' Committee:
AVCC Guidelines for Quality Assurance in University Course Development and Review
http://www.avcc.edu.au/avcc/pubs/glquass.htm

Graduate Careers Council of Australia
http://rubens.its.unimelb.edu.au/~rbb/

The International Network for Quality in Higher Education
http://nica.marstu.mari.su/INQAAHE.htm

J.M. Consulting, HEFCE Publication[1]

The relevance of higher education to future employment

The QA exercise emphasises the expectation that higher education should have relevance to future employment needs. In higher education, this expectation has brought to prominence the term 'transferable skills' and 'key skills'.

But the whole notion of transferable skills is the cause of considerable debate in higher education – and is still something of an unknown quantity as far as many lecturers are concerned. So, what are transferable skills? Are they already part and parcel of the courses you are involved in? Could they be? Should they be? If yes, what can you do to help develop them?

One useful way of looking at 'transferable skills' is to put them into a broader context of skills, as shown in Figure 1.3 below.

Figure 1.3   An analysis of skills development

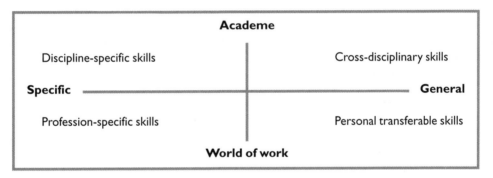

Source: Barnett (1994)[2]

For the most part, degree courses focus on discipline-specific skills. Some may include profession-specific skills, particularly those with a clear vocational element, validated by professional bodies (eg health sciences, aspects of engineering, law, architecture). Many degree programmes will pay some attention to more broad-based academic skills (eg literature searching; academic writing; developing skills of critique and analysis) – although there is often an assumption that these skills will be developed 'naturally'. But until recently, only a minority of degree programmes have actively explored how to help students develop general skills relevant to the world of work – ie 'transferable skills'.

Activity 1C below and overleaf gives some examples of transferable skills, plus space for you to make a note of those you think might be appropriate in the areas you teach. The list is not exhaustive: feel free to add to it.

Activity 1C   Assessing what 'transferable skills' you help students to develop

Transferable skills	Examples	Tick the skills you actively help students to develop
Communication	Writing reports, giving presentations, using media	
Group work	Leadership, chairing meetings, team work, delegating	
Personal	Independence, autonomy, self-assessment, self-confidence	
Interpersonal	Influencing, counselling, listening, interviewing, assertiveness, negotiation	
Organizational	Time management, project management, objective setting, project evaluation	
IT	Word processing, database, graphics, DTP, spreadsheets	

Transferable skills	Examples	Tick the skills you actively help students to develop
Information gathering	Locating information sources, evaluating data sources, extracting information, analysing information, presenting data	
Learning	Flexible reading, note taking, literature review	

Source: Gibbs et al (1994)[3]

Feedback

If you have ticked several items in this list, check the publicity material for your courses, and talk to students – do they know they are developing these skills? Are they encouraged to make use of them in their final year when submitting job applications? Many courses may include 'transferable skills' but fail to make them explicit to anyone! If you have only ticked a few items, think about whether you can and should include a wider range. This pack does not attempt to address all these skills. However, it may be useful, especially for the last three items on this list.

1.1.3 The impact of technology on the acquisition of knowledge

Another growing pressure for change in higher education is the impact which new technologies are having on the acquisition and dissemination of knowledge. Put crudely, the knowledge base in many disciplines is multiplying exponentially.

This leaves the 'teacher' with a growing challenge of working out what to include in a course of study. Many people accept that it is no longer possible or useful to encourage students to 'learn' a given body of information. Instead, it is the teacher's job to facilitate student exploration of a field, helping students to develop a basic grounding in a subject, and enabling them to become adept at exploring new avenues for themselves.

Work through Activity 1D to estimate for yourself the impact that technological developments have had on your access to new developments in your discipline. To what extent has your access to information in your subject area changed in the past five years?

Activity 1D   Analysing the impact of technology on your access to information in your specialist area

Facility	I used this five years ago	I use this today	I'd like to use this but...
Text-based bibliographic search			
On-line searching done by library staff			
CD-ROM bibliographies			
On-line bibliographic search by self			
Communicating by email with research colleagues outside my university			
'Surfing' the Internet			
Journals available electronically			
Teleconferencing			

Feedback

If you have put any ticks in the last column, you might like to explore the technology sections that look at the practicalities of using information technology.

✗	Technology in Teaching	2	How to get connected to the Internet
		3	Using Internet resources
		4	Communicating using computers
		5	Using the World Wide Web
✗	Using Technology	4.2	Communicating via email
		4.3	Participating in electronic discussion groups
		3.4.1	Some examples of computer-delivered resources

You may also like to reflect on whether changes in access to information have changed what you teach.

1.1.4 *Developments in educational research*

In addition to changes in the student body, public expectations of higher education and technological advances, there have been developments in our understanding of the nature of teaching and learning within the higher education sector. Research into higher education, as compared with compulsory education, has been quite limited. It is now growing in momentum, as the calls for 'public accountability', 'quality', and definitions of 'standards' have risen.

It is not the aim of this package to give a detailed analysis of theories and models of teaching and learning. However, it is worth looking at a limited range of underlying concepts about teaching and learning, in order to give a framework for thinking about educational development.

We have already briefly explored one view of what 'educational quality' looks like, from the perspective of the Higher Education Funding Council (see 1.1.2 in this section). How well does this fit with your own views? Think back to your own university experience, pick out a part of that experience which you felt was particularly successful and note down your answers to the questions in Activity 1E.

Activity 1E   **Exploring a positive experience of higher education**

What was the experience?

How did it feel?

What evidence did you have that it was 'successful'?

What do you think it was that made it successful?

Now use that example to start to define what, for you, constitutes 'effective' teaching and learning at the higher education level. Again, you may find it helpful to record your thoughts here:

Feedback

Compare what you have written down with the following list, which gives some indication of what learners are looking for from their teachers.

Figure 1.4 *Most popular qualities of lecturers according to graduate students*

Mastery of subject, competent	717
Lectures well prepared	712
Subject related to life, practical	555
Students' questions and opinions encouraged	481
Enthusiastic about subject	385
Approachable, friendly, available	372
Concerned for student progress	325
Had sense of humour, amusing	321
Sought social contact with students	27
Interested in student activities	15
Mature, wise	8

Humanities graduates emphasized sense of humour, enthusiasm and encouragement of student questions, while physical & biological science graduates emphasized items relating to planning and the orderly organization of the course.

Source: Sheffield (ed) (1974) *Teaching in the universities: no one way*[4]

There is general agreement that 'effective teaching' is 'that which enables effective learning'. Which leads us on to ask: 'So what is effective learning?' And, for university teachers: 'What is effective learning in higher education?' Is it about learning facts, accumulating and organizing information, understanding concepts, developing powers of critical reasoning, developing complex skills, or developing particular attitudes?

One helpful model of learning at higher education level is Diana Laurillard's 'conversational framework' (see Figure 1.5). This model sees higher education as having two key components. On the one hand, there is the development of conceptual understanding – essentially thought processes focused on knowledge/ideas/information/concepts. On the other hand, there are skills – essentially actions/ways of behaving/doing/competencies. Degree programmes may balance these two components in different ways: the challenge is to work out what approaches to teaching and learning enable students to develop these key components.

Figure 1.5   The conversational framework

Teacher

operating at a
conceptual level

process of dialogue whereby both sides adapt concepts in the light of each other's description

Student

operating at a
conceptual level

process of adapting
and subsequently
further modifying
tasks in the light of
student description
and action

process of adapting
and subsequently
further modifying
tasks in the light of
tutor feedback

operating at the 'real
world' level of action

process of action/reflection associated with tasks set by tutor and adapted in the light of student feedback

operating at the 'real
world' level of action

adapted from: Laurillard (1993) *Rethinking university teaching*[5]

Laurillard (1993) '*Balancing the media*'[6]

In seeking to understand the learning process further, it is worth focusing on the different roles which can be adopted by the key players – the teacher/lecturer/ learning facilitator (for convenience we shall use the term 'tutor') and the learner or student.

Exploring the role of the tutor

The role of the tutor depends on a range of factors, including your own personal views and experience of education, the system within which you are working and the students with whom you are working. One important factor is the extent to which you feel you should control the learning process. 'Control' ranges from determining what students learn, how that learning is structured, and what approaches to learning are made available, to whose job it is to motivate learning, how the outcomes of learning are judged and by whom.

Activity 1F gives you an opportunity to explore how much responsibility for their learning you are prepared to give your students.

Activity 1F Attitudes towards increasing learner responsibility

Indicate your feelings about each of the following statements by circling the appropriate response. Rather than basing your response on a generalized group of university students, you may find it more valuable to work through it first with a specific first-year undergraduate class in mind, and then thinking about a final-year class or postgraduate students.

	Strongly agree				Strongly disagree
When opportunities exist for learners to work or study on their own they learn more effectively	5	4	3	2	1
Even though attempts are made to give learners significant responsibility for their own learning, most seldom take advantage of those opportunities	1	2	3	4	5
On their own, learners generally accomplish goals which they participate in setting	5	4	3	2	1
Learners gain from opportunities to participate in determining criteria for accomplishing goals that have been set	5	4	3	2	1
Lecturers should closely supervise their students to facilitate efficient learning	1	2	3	4	5
When learners participate in setting their own expectations, there is a positive interaction between lecturer and learner	5	4	3	2	1
Learners have a high regard for lecturers who direct them systematically step by step through the learning process	1	2	3	4	5
Allowing learners to control their own time usually results in the appropriate use of that time	5	4	3	2	1
Allowing learners to assume control of their own learning causes confusion	1	2	3	4	5
Most learners do not understand the rationale for participating in setting their own learning expectations	1	2	3	4	5

	Strongly agree				Strongly disagree
When learners are given more responsibility for their own learning they are more likely to accomplish that learning	5	4	3	2	1
Learners can profitably evaluate the learning and performance of their peers	5	4	3	2	1
Learners can usually not provide constructive feedback to their peers after evaluating their learning	1	2	3	4	5
Learners who are personally committed to goals and expectations set by the lecturer will require little supervision	5	4	3	2	1
Most learners will make decisions about their own learning and their own conduct in a manner that benefits both the course on which they are working and their peers	5	4	3	2	1
Lecturers should generally observe their learners as they fulfil their responsibilities	1	2	3	4	5
Learners should be evaluated frequently by the lecturer to determine whether they are performing adequately	1	2	3	4	5
Lecturers should plan their learners' schedules and assign responsibilities	1	2	3	4	5
Lecturers should be the principal source of evaluation for any learner	1	2	3	4	5
Learners can constructively evaluate their own learning and/or performance	5	4	3	2	1

Total score:

Enter your scores onto the scale below.

20 _____ 100

Source: Stritter (1986)[7]

Feedback

If you fall close to the left-hand end of the scale, then you see yourself or lecturers in general as playing a crucial role in enabling students to learn. Without you, students will not know where to go, what to do, how they are progressing, or when they have 'achieved'. You might like to reflect on why you hold this view of students, and on your role in their learning (reflect back to when you were a student yourself). Many of the suggestions put forward in this book are concerned with shifting responsibility for learning quite considerably from you to your students. It will be important for you to consider how you feel about this, and to consult colleagues who have confidence in working this way. It will also certainly be worth your while reading the case studies used to illustrate particular methods.

If, on the other hand, your score falls close to the right-hand end of the scale, you see learners as being able and willing to take responsibility for themselves. They can set their own goals, and give and receive feedback to and from each other. Your role is primarily to encourage, to ensure that resources and facilities are adequate, and to be a reference point for your students. This book supports this approach to learning, so we hope you will find some suggestions that will help you strengthen this approach.

In Activity 1F you may have found that you were prepared to be 'less controlling' with final-year students or postgraduates than with first-year students. In this context, the concept of 'learning phases' is worth considering. One classification of learning suggests that it goes through the following phases:

Phases of learning	Approaches to teaching
Orienting Motivating Presenting	These are often approached in a fairly 'controlled' way through lectures and prescribed reading. In the conversational model (see section 1.1.4 above), this is shown by the communication from teacher to student at the concept level.
Clarifying Elaborating Consolidating Confirming	These are achieved necessarily by a much more interactive approach – which requires that the student has ample opportunity to test ideas, put them into action and get feedback on them. In the 'conversational model' (Figure 1.5) this is shown by the feedback loops, both at the concept level and at the action level.

This does not mean that first-year students are only working through the first three phases, but early on the emphasis is more likely to be focused on basic orientation and presentation.

Three further concepts worth highlighting in the context of the role of the tutor are active learning, flexible learning and co-operative learning.

Passive learning is where the student acts or is treated as an 'empty vessel' into which knowledge can be poured. A classic example is where students take copious notes from formal lectures; simply copying from words and visuals produced by the tutor and then regurgitate this material, more or less unaltered, in essays and exam answers. In contrast, *active learning* involves tutor and learner engaging in the learning process together with the learner taking an active role in understanding the ideas presented, seeking out new avenues to explore and playing a part in judging their own progress. Many of the ideas in this pack focus on teaching approaches which should encourage active learning. Another useful source of ideas is the series *Effective learning and teaching in higher education*.

Cryer (1992) *Effective learning and teaching in higher education*[8]

Flexible and Independent learning is about shifting the whole culture of learning further down the continuum of learner control. It moves away from large group approaches towards courses aimed at giving individuals far more control over content and outcomes. Flexible learning often involves individual learners in establishing their own learning contracts, guides them to appropriate resources, engages them in self and peer assessment and focuses in many cases on real life problems and action. Many of the ideas in the Teaching and Learning chapters may be adapted to support flexible learning approaches. In this case, IT offers an ideal way of giving students access to resources, as well as to individual and individualized learning activities.

Using Technology   3   Using computers to deliver teaching and learning resources

Within the framework of flexible and independent learning, you often find an emphasis on *co-operative or collaborative learning* – where small groups of learners may be providing as much support and guidance to each other as does the tutor. Again, IT has demonstrated its role here – with the development of 'computer-supported co-operative learning'.

Using Technology   4   Using computers to communicate with and between students

For more on these teaching and learning concepts:

Teaching and learning in an expanding higher education system: report of a working party of the Committee of Scottish University Principals[9]

McConnell (1994), *Implementing computer-supported co-operative learning*[10]

Exploring the role of the student

Research into student learning indicates that there are individual differences in terms of how students approach their learning. Here, two sets of concepts are worth highlighting: deep versus surface learning and holistic vs serialist learners.

Deep learning and surface learning

Surface learning, as the name suggests, applies to learning where the student takes on board ideas coming from the teacher, but does not then 'translate' or adapt those ideas in any way. The extreme version of this is rote learning. Surface learning is essentially about reproducing knowledge or skills without much understanding. Students who adopt this approach will tend to find higher education more and more difficult as they meet concepts which require them to integrate different aspects of their knowledge base. They also face many problems in applying knowledge to action, or adapting skills from one setting to another.

In contrast, deep learning applies to learning where students actively seek to understand new ideas, integrate these with what they already know and test them on reality.

Deep learning and surface learning may represent individual differences in learning styles, but they are also influenced by learning opportunities and assessment methods. For example, students who have heavy lecture-based or laboratory class timetables, with an emphasis on assessment requiring them to memorize large volumes of information, may adopt a surface learning approach simply to survive. The surface learner is more likely than the deep learner to take a passive learner role. Surface learners may require careful tutor support if faced with courses that encourage them to take a lot of responsibility for their own learning.

Holistic learners and serialist learners

Another distinction made between learners is the 'holistic'/'serialist' dimension. Holists like to start with the 'big picture' and then explore the details as their grasp of the overall picture takes shape. Serialists prefer information and ideas to be introduced gradually, enabling them to build up the picture as they might piece together a jigsaw. These two approaches indicate the need for tutors to adapt how they present ideas in the first place, to accommodate these different needs.

Going Deep
An article from The National Teaching & Learning Forum. This is an online newsletter from educators to educators sharing new ways of helping students improve their learning.
http://www.ntlf.com/html/pi/9512/article2.htm

Deep/Surface Approaches To Learning: An Introduction
James Rhem, Executive Editor
An article from The National Teaching & Learning Forum
http://www.ntlf.com/html/pi/9512/article1.htm

Explorations in Learning and Instruction: the theory in practice database
Dr. Greg Kearsley
This is a comprehensive database outlining instructional theories.
http://www.gwu.edu/~tip/

Higher Education Development International
From this website you can find: models of teaching and learning in higher education, what's happening in universities around the world, how educational development units operate and information about conferences and publications.
http://www.abo.fi/hied/

Engines for Educators
Roger Schank
This is a comprehensive online book looking at learning within schools.
http://www.ils.nwu.edu/~e_for_e/nodes/I-M-NODE-4121-pg.html

1.1.5 *Conclusions*

The key points arising from the literature on teaching and learning are that:

1 Tutors need to develop a range of teaching strategies – in order to take into account the different learning styles of their students.

2 The emphasis should be on active approaches which encourage learners not simply to take on board ideas and skills, but to adapt and integrate them into their own ways of thinking and behaving.

3 Teaching should be a two-way (at least!) communication process – enabling adaptation on both sides. There is evidence that there is much to be gained from student–student communication as well as student–tutor communication.

4 Learning should incorporate not only knowledge and work at the conceptual level, but also skills – with the inclusion in courses of ample practical activities aimed at developing those skills.

Diana Laurillard has explored in some depth the extent to which different media are able to replace or augment the role of the teacher in the learning process. Figure 1.6 summarizes her findings, which suggest that:

- media can certainly 'replace' teachers to achieve certain aspects of the learning process; but, for the most part, to ensure that all aspects of the learning process are addressed the teacher will continue to have a crucial role to play

- she sees some potential for 'intelligent tutoring systems' and 'tutor simulations' to fulfil all aspects of support for the learning process – but acknowledges the complexity, cost and time required to develop these systems.

Figure 1.6 *Media comparison chart*

	Print	Audio-vision	Television	Video	Self-assessed questions	Hypertext	Multimedia resources	Simulation	Microworld	Modelling	Tutorial program	Tutoring system	Tutorial simulation	Audio conferencing	Video conferencing	Computer conferencing	Computer-supported collaborative work
1 T can describe conception	✔	✔	✔	✔	–	✔	✔	–	–	–	✔	✔	✔	✔	✔	✔	–
2 S can describe conception	–	✔	–	–	✔	✔	✔	–	✔	✔	✔	✔	✔	✔	✔	✔	✔
3 T can redescribe in light of S's conception or action	–	–	–	–	–	–	–	–	–	–	✔	✔	✔	✔	✔	✔	–
4 S can redescribe in light of T's redescription or action	–	✔	–	–	✔	✔	✔	–	–	–	✔	✔	✔	–	–	–	–
5 T can adapt task goal in light of S's description or action	–	–	–	–	–	–	–	–	–	–	✔	✔	✔	–	–	–	–
6 T can set task goal	–	✔	✔	✔	✔	–	–	✔	✔	✔	✔	✔	✔	–	–	–	✔
7 S can act to achieve task goal	–	✔	–	–	✔	–	✔	✔	✔	✔	✔	✔	✔	✔	–	–	✔
8 T can set up world to give intrinsic feedback on actions	–	✔	✔	✔	–	–	✔	✔	✔	✔	–	✔	✔	–	–	–	✔
9 S can modify action in light of intrinsic feedback on action	–	✔	–	–	–	–	✔	✔	✔	✔	–	✔	✔	–	–	–	✔
10 S can adapt actions in light of T's description of S's redescription	–	✔	–	–	✔	–	–	–	–	✔	✔	✔	✔	–	–	–	✔
11 S can reflect on interaction to modify description	–	✔	–	✔	✔	–	✔	–	✔	✔	–	✔	✔	–	–	–	✔
12 T can reflect on S's action to modify redescription	–	–	–	–	–	–	–	–	–	–	✔	✔	✔	–	–	–	–

Adapted from: Laurillard (1993) *Rethinking university teaching*[11]

Since the late 1980s the main parameters within which university teaching staff have operated have changed radically. A simple answer to: 'Why change how we teach?' is: 'In order to survive'. A more positive response is: 'To ensure that the undergraduates and postgraduates of today receive as good an education as we ourselves did'.

1.2 What are the options for change?

To every problem or challenge in higher education, different people and different perspectives will produce different solutions. Some of the strategies for addressing the current challenges facing higher education are outlined below.

1.2.1 Some strategies

Finding ways of adapting or refining 'traditional' methods of teaching to suit the needs of a 'mass' higher education system with reduced resources

In the early 1990s the UK Polytechnics and Colleges Funding Council commissioned a project entitled 'Teaching more students'. One product of this was a series of A4 booklets and an accompanying video for use either by individuals or to support staff development workshops. The pack highlighted ways of developing and improving on lectures, discussion sessions and assessment, as well as introducing ideas about resource-based learning. These booklets provide university teachers with a range of suggestions on how to cope with large numbers without compromising quality.

The project has now ended, but the materials are still available from the Oxford Centre for Staff Development.[12]

Finding 'new' ways of teaching – where 'new' may be a case of either adapting forms of education already proven in other sectors, or radically rethinking the nature and process of education

An obvious example of 'new' developments is making greater use of IT on which this book focuses. As a result of a range of UK government initiatives on IT in Higher Education the number of examples of the use of computers is growing. Examples include to

- support/augment and in some cases replace (in part) the role of the tutor in the learning process

- tackle problems of communication between tutors and students, and between students

- provide students with greater or easier access to learning resources – without the need for major expansions in book and journal provision in university libraries.

In the following section we look at each of these approaches in more detail. Another example worth mentioning is the Enterprise in Higher Education initiative. Here 'new' approaches of teaching and learning have been explored through creating a bridge between universities and industry. This has provided students with opportunities for developing their skills in work settings.

Biggs, Brighton, Minnit, Pow and Wicksteed '*Thematic Evaluation of EHEI*' [13]

Exploring ways of decreasing 'costs' of teaching, without jeopardising quality

Some universities are looking towards US models of university education, whereby much of the face-to-face contact with undergraduates is undertaken by graduate teaching assistants (GTAs) rather than by full-time academic staff, and where much greater use is made of student self-help groups. At first sight this may seem like a cost-cutting exercise which is bound to affect quality. However, where GTAs are appropriately trained, where academics can develop skills as managers/enablers of learning rather than face-to-face teachers, and where adequate support is given to the student self-help groups, this approach can produce very positive results.

 Using Technology   4.2   Communicating via email

Another possibility here is to explore the potential of distance and open learning – where face-to-face contact between tutors and students is substantially reduced, being replaced by other media (such as print, video, audio-tape or computer-assisted learning). More and more traditional universities are starting to experiment with this approach, which until recently had been the monopoly (at HE level in the UK) of the Open University.

 Using Technology   4.6   Considerations for open and distance learning courses

There are doubtless many other strategies which could be considered. The brief notes above simply highlight a range of important developments that are being explored. This pack focuses on only one of these options – although it will also have a role to play in others. The purpose of presenting these options is to highlight that IT is not 'the only' or necessarily 'the best' option – but is one of a range of options to be considered, evaluated and incorporated into the best aspects of current practice.

If you decide that greater use of IT may be the way you want to go, you will find on the following pages a range of useful contacts in support of IT developments in higher education. The one other matter to pay careful attention to is copyright and intellectual property rights. Do not let such issues put you off exploring the potential of IT in HE – but do be aware that if you get heavily involved in developments in this area, you are likely to need expert advice and support on aspects such as what material you may use and for what purposes.

1.2.2 *What support is there for IT developments?*

Acknowledgement of the potential of IT in teaching and learning can be seen by a number of UK government initiatives which have set out to explore, develop and evaluate ways of encouraging teaching and learning. The starting point, in the late 1980s, was to develop the necessary IT skills for designing and developing teaching materials (ITTI: Information Technology Training Initiative). The next stage involved setting up centres to support developments in specific disciplines (CTI: Computers in Teaching Initiative). This then developed to active support in the form of a broad range of initiatives aimed at developing both subject specialist courseware, and more broadly-based institutional programmes aimed at incorporating developments in IT into teaching across institutions (TLTP: Teaching and Learning Technology Programme). This section provides a brief overview of the initiatives, and gives contact addresses which were current in 1995. You will be able to find more up-to-date information on the World Wide Web.

Technology in Teaching   1.4   What kinds of material can you put on the computer?

Information Technology Training Initiative (ITTI)

ITTI came into existence in 1991. Its aim was to improve the availability of training materials for the use of IT in UK higher education institutions. Funding (of about £3 million) was made available over three years to support training developments. The initiative has funded 29 projects in universities throughout the UK. These projects are in the main producing quality paper-based and computer-based products in areas such as:

- IT application skills training (such as geographical information systems, statistics and graphics)
- basic IT skills
- multimedia and hypertext courseware development tools and training
- professional IT skills training for UNIX, X-Windows and networking.

If you want further information about the products of this initiative, contact UCoSDA (Universities' and Colleges' Staff Development Agency).[14]

Additional background information can be obtained from the ITTI national co-ordinator, Brian Shields.

ITTI World Wide Web home page
http://www.icbl.hw.ac.uk/itti

UCoSDA World Wide Web home page
http://www.niss.ac.uk/education/ucosda.html

The Computers in Teaching Initiative (CTI)

CTI is funded by the Higher Education Funding Councils for England, Scotland and Wales, and the Department for Education Northern Ireland. Its aim is to transform university teaching by introducing the possibilities of information technology to lecturers, raising their awareness of what can be achieved by using computers as a tool for learning and evaluating the educational potential of IT in UK universities.

The current phase of the initiative began in 1989 with the establishment of 19 CTI centres (four more were added later). Each centre is responsible for a different subject area and works within its discipline community to provide a support and information service tailored to the needs of that discipline. Centres are directed by experienced university academics and staffed by subject specialists with expertise in learning technology. The centres are co-ordinated and supported by the CTI Support Service (CTISS) based at the University of Oxford.

CTI centres:
- produce regular newsletters
- publish resource guides and review courseware
- provide on-line information via JANET
- run workshops and conferences
- visit university departments to demonstrate software and advise on computers in teaching
- answer individual enquiries.

Here are the subject areas which have a CTI centre:

CTI Accounting, Finance & Management
CTI Biology
CTI Centre for the Built Environment
CTI Centre for Chemistry
CTI Centre for Computing
CTI Centre for Economics
CTI Engineering
CTI Centre for Geography, Geology & Meteorology
CTI Centre for History, Archaeology & Art History
CTI Human Services
CTI Centre for Land Use & Environmental Sciences
CTI Centre for Law

CTI Centre for Library & Information Studies
CTI Mathematics
CTI Centre for Medicine
CTI Centre for Modern Languages (with Classics)
CTI Music
CTI Nursing and Midwifery
CTI Centre for Physics
CTI Psychology
CTI Centre for Sociology & the Policy Sciences
CTI Centre for Statistics
CTI Centre for Textual Studies
CTI Support Service

CTI Homepage
   http://info.ox.ac.uk/cti/index.html

For further details contact , Joyce Martin or Sue Peacock at CTISS.[15]

The Teaching and Learning Technology Programme (TLTP)

The stated aim of TLTP is 'to make teaching and learning more productive and efficient by harnessing modern technology'. In 1992 the Universities Funding Council (UFC) allocated £7.5 million a year over three years to the programme. It invited bids from universities for funding projects to develop new methods of teaching and learning through the use of technology. Some 43 projects received funding under this first phase. Around a quarter of these projects are addressing problems of implementation within single institutions, with staff development being a major component. The remainder of the projects are concerned with courseware development and involve academics from different institutions working in consortia. The size of consortia range from two to 44 members and the projects cover a wide range of subject disciplines.

In April 1993 the new funding bodies, HEFCE, HEFCW, SHEFC and DENI agreed jointly to fund a second phase of the programme. This phase was launched with the same aim as the first but with the intention of building on the work already being undertaken by the Phase 1 projects. In 1993 a further 33 projects were funded, with a budget in 1993–94 of £3.75 million.

It has always been envisaged by the funding bodies that both phases of the programme should run for up to three years, and most institutions submitted bids for funding over a two- to three-year period. The HEFCE, HEFCW and DENI have agreed, in principle, to fund the programme for the full term, subject to a review of the funds available in 1994–95 and 1995–96.

For further information about TLTP contact TLTP projects officer, Emma Greenwood or Sarah Turpin, the National Coordinator at TLTP.[16]

TLTP Central Web
   http://www.tltp.ac.uk:UK/tltp

In the United States there is no exact replica of the above initiatives. There are however associations, centres and consortia offering help to individuals and institutions, where the thrust is 'working together'. The American Association of Higher Education (AAHE) has both institutional and individual members who look at the wider issues of higher education within society. They have a technology section offering a variety of projects. One of these projects is the 'Teaching, Learning & Technology (TLT) Round Table Program'. It is a programme that provides a conceptual framework to improve teaching and learning through technology. It helps institutions set up round tables and work with peer institutions.

American Association of Higher Education (AAHE) Homepage
http://www.aahe.org/

The Maricopa Center for Learning and Instruction (MCLI) at Maricopa Community Colleges. This centre is considered a national model for enthusing and motivating staff towards teaching and learning innovation. They are interested in communities learning together and have set up the 'Ocotillo' project along the lines of the AAHE round table program where faculties within the Maricopa community colleges come together to discuss teaching and learning innovations outside the normal committee structures. Their site contains a wealth of information on teaching using the World Wide Web (a page where you will find over 468 examples of the Web being used for teaching and learning with technology).

Maricopa Centre for Learning and Instruction Homepage
http://www.mcli.dist.maricopa.edu/

Educom is a non-profit consortium of higher educational institutions with a similar community spirit to the those above. Their corporate leadership partners are IBM and Apple computers. Educom aims to help its members understand the significant role that technology will play in education in the future. They offer seminars, publications and specialized groups such the 'National Learning Infrastructure Inititiave' (NLII) and the 'Network and Telecommunications Task Force' (NTTF).

Educom Homepage
http://www.educom.edu/

In Australia the Committee for University Teaching and Staff Development have been funded for three years (1996–1999) to promote teaching excellence in higher education. They have set up a 'National Teaching Development Grants and Staff Development Grants'. The National Teaching and Development Grants operate at both the individual and organizational level. The Committee are also administering the UniServe project that disseminates information and innovative material about university teaching and learning. The Australian Vice-Chancellors' Committee has also issued a paper on the exploitation of IT within higher education which gives an official view of the area.

The Committee for University Teaching and Staff Development (CUTSD) Homepage
http://uniserve.edu.au/CUTSD/

Uniserve
http://uniserve.edu.au/uniserve/

AVCC (Australian Vice Chancellors' Committee) **Exploiting Information Technology in Higher Education: an issues paper 9 October 1996**
http://www.avcc.edu.au/avcc/pubs/eitihe.htm

1.3 Copyright and intellectual property rights

If, after working through this pack you decide to embark on producing multimedia courseware, you will need to spend some time looking into the legal minefield of copyright. For your own sake and that of your institution, it is also worth becoming more familiar with intellectual property rights – the rights accruing to you as a producer of computer courseware. This section outlines the key points to consider in these areas. You will then need to add to this – see the suggested reading at the end of this section– and to explore what legal advice is available in your institution, together a wide range of media from different sources. The disadvantage of this is that as soon as you start bringing these materials together to make them available to colleagues and students, you will need to get copyright permission for them. And the problem with this is that each type of material is protected by different pieces of legislation, and different systems for obtaining permission to use it.

What is covered by copyright?
The answer to this is virtually everything. Nine different types of work are protected by copyright:

-   literary works (including letters, memos, directories, song lyrics, computer programs, computer codes)
-   dramatic works (including stage directions, instructions for dance and mime)
-   musical works (scores, directions)
-   artistic works (including photographs, sculptures, some architecture and artistic craftsmanship)
-   sound recordings
-   films
-   broadcasts (including satellite)
-   cable programmes
-   published editions (including layout and typography)

In addition, there are performers' rights – relevant to several of the types of work listed above (for instance films, broadcasts, sound recordings).

What do you need to do to get copyright clearance?

In seeking copyright clearance for each of these, you need to be clear about who owns the copyright and what the terms of the copyright are. You then need to contact the owner of the copyright, or 'collecting societies' who act on behalf of copyright owners, explaining how you intend to use the material.

While the general principle is that copyright is owned by the 'creator' of the work, it can be sold or passed on. Publishers' own published editions of published materials such as books or dramatic works. In addition, work produced as part of employment is often owned by the employer rather than by the creator.

The terms of copyright on different types of work vary considerably, and are influenced by different copyright laws, the main ones being the 1911 Act, the 1956 Act and the 1988 Act. Terms vary from 25 years for published editions to the author's life and 70 years after his or her death for literary works.

One thing to watch out for is that copyright law differs from country to country, so if you are producing materials which will be available outside the UK, you will need to be sure they do not contravene copyright laws elsewhere. Once you have established who owns the copyright, you need to contact the owner to ask permission to use the material, giving the following information:

- the title of the new work, and its aims
- a description of the target audience
- a description of how it will be distributed (eg commercially or not for profit) and the geographical coverage of the expected marketing
- the name of the publisher/distributor dealing with the new work.

Tracking down the individual copyright owner is often difficult. It is worth starting by contacting the most relevant 'collecting society' to see if the copyright owner is registered there. If so, the staff can advise you about terms and conditions of use, and payment where this is required. These are some of the collecting societies:

- British Phonographic Industry
- Christian Copyright Licensing
- Copyright Licensing Agency
- Design and Artistic Copyright Society
- International Federation of Phonographic Industries
- Mechanical Copyright Protection Society
- The Ordnance Survey
- Performing Rights Society

   –   Phonographic Performance Ltd

   –   Video Performance Ltd.

For further information about these and other collecting societies, contact the Copyright Licensing Agency.[17]

The important point to remember is that the onus is on **you** to obtain copyright clearance. It takes time and effort: it is not something to be done late in the day, when you are about to get your courseware duplicated and distributed. As you prepare material, keep a log of anything which may need clearance, and start finding out where you need to apply to get it. In seeking clearance, it is probably better to think quite ambitiously about how the material will end up being used and distributed than to start by asking for clearance to use material for a limited audience, and then realize later on that you want to market it worldwide. Each time you broaden the reach of your new work, you will need to get new clearance.

To obtain clearance if you are living in the UK, telephone the Copyright Licensing Agency.[17] You will need to ask for a licence (many of the collecting agencies will be able to supply these), and you should ensure that you have written agreement about the rights being made available to you.

1.3.1 *Intellectual property rights and licensing*

Once you have produced some courseware yourself, and obtained the relevant copyright agreements from third parties to allow you to use their materials in the ways stated in the licences, you will also need to take steps to protect your own rights over the new work.

This will include establishing how you want to handle the material. Will you market and distribute it yourself, or hand over to a commercial operator the task (and some of the rights with it) of producing and distributing the materials?

If you go for marketing and distributing your own work, then you will retain the copyright. You will need to establish a licensing agreement of your own, which indicates how people purchasing your material can use it. It is definitely worth contacting a legal adviser for guidance in drawing up your licensing agreement.

If you hand your material over to a commercial publisher, then you are essentially selling or assigning your copyright to the publisher, and need to be sure that you will receive adequate payment from the publisher in return. Again, legal advice here is important.

The above notes have been adapted from *Copyright guidelines for the Teaching and Learning Technology Programme*. The booklet also includes examples of licensing agreements, a wide range of contact addresses, and useful suggestions on how to keep a log of copyright material you wish to use.

TLTP (1994) *Copyright guidelines for the Teaching and Learning Technology Programme*[18]

For those living in the United States, there are several good websites to visit for information. For a chatty introduction to some of the myths of copyright issues try Brad Templeton's website: **10 Big Myths about Copyright**. The **Copyright Web** explains the fundamentals of copyright law in the United States, explaining terms like: copyhoarding, licensing, copylefting, freeware and shareware. The complex nature of copyright for multimedia education has brought 'fair use' into sharp focus. You can find out more about this at: **Fair Use Guidelines for Educational Multimedia**. This is an association that has kept in touch with the Committee on Fair Use of Educational Media, begun as an initiative of 'The Consortium of College and University Media Centers'. This website gives you access to the Multimedia Fair Use Document. The **Institute for Learning Technologies (ILT) Web** is a very comprehensive site on the legal issues of copyright (please note the authors do not see this as a site for legal advice). The site covers areas such as: copyright basics (eg types of work covered, intellectual property protection, how to copyright your work), court cases, copyright and education and copyright and multmedia. Finally, once you have decided to go ahead, you can try the **Copyright Clearance Center, Inc,** which is a non-profit making organization set up to help those seeking copyright clearance.

If you live in Australia, see the **Australian Copyright Council**. This website offers, for example, information, publication and free legal advice.

10 Big Myths about Copyright
http://www.clari.net/brad/copymyths.html

Copyright Web
http://www.benedict.com/

Fair Use Guidelines for Educational Multimedia
http://www.libraries.psu.edu/avs/fairuse/

Institute for Learning Technologies (ILT) Web
http://www.ilt.columbia.edu/projects/copyright/index.html

Copyright Clearance Center, Inc
http://www.copyright.com/

Australian Copyright Council
http://www.copyright.org.au/

References for Chapter 1

[1] J.M. Consulting (1997), *International Comparison of Teaching Cost*, HEFCE Publication HEFCE, Northan House, Coldharbour Lane, Bristol BS16 1QD, UK

[2] Barnett, R. (1994), *The limits of competence: knowledge, higher education and society*, SRHE

[3] Gibbs, G., C. Rust, A. Jenkins and D. Jaques (1994), *Developing students' transferable skills*, Oxford Centre for Staff Development

[4] Sheffield, E. (ed) (1974), *Teaching in the universities: no one way*, McGill-Queens University Press, Montreal

[5] Laurillard, Diana (1993), *Rethinking university teaching: a framework for the effective use of educational technology*, Routledge, London, p. 103

[6] Laurillard, Diana (1993), 'Balancing the media', *Journal of educational technology*, vol. 19 no. 2, pp 81–93

[7] Stritter, Frank T. (1986), Attitudes to increasing learner responsibility questionnaire (personal communication), contact Frank Stritter, University of North Carolina, Chapel Hill, North Carolina, USA.

[8] Cryer, Pat (1992), *Effective learning and teaching in higher education* series, CVCP, Universities' Staff Development Unit, Sheffield

[9] *Teaching and learning in an expanding higher education system*: Report of a Working Party of the Committee of Scottish University Principals

[10] McConnell, David (1994), *Implementing computer-supported co-operative learning*, Kogan Page, London

[11] Laurillard, Diana (1993), *Rethinking university teaching: a framework for the effective use of educational technology*, Routledge, London, p. 177

[12] Oxford Centre for Staff Development, Gipsy Lane Campus, Headington, Oxford OX3 0BP, tel. 01865 750918, fax: 01865 744437, email: ocsd@brookesss.ac.uk

[13] Biggs, Brighton, Minnit, Pow and Wicksteed *Thematic Evaluation of EHEI* Employment Department Sheffield 1994

[14] UCoSDA, Ingram House, 65 Wilkinson Street, University of Sheffield, Sheffield S10 3GJ, England, tel: 0114 272 5248, fax: 0114 272 8705, email: ucosda@sheffield.ac.uk

[15] Joyce Martin; Head of CTISS; Manager; Sue Peacock, Administrator; Chris Edwards, Secretary; CTI Support Service, University of Oxford, 13 Banbury Road, Oxford OX2 6NN, England, tel: 01865 273273, fax: 01865 273275, email: CTISS@oucs.ox.ac.uk

[16] Sarah Turpin, TLTP National Co-ordinator; Northavon House, Coldharbour Lane, Bristol BS16 1QD, England, tel: 0117 931 7454, fax: 0117 931 7173, email: tltp@hefce.ac.uk

[17] The Copyright Licensing Agency, 90 Tottenham Court Road, London W1P 9HE, England, tel: 0171 436 5931, fax: 0171 436 3986.

[18] TLTP (1994), *Copyright guidelines for the Teaching and Learning Technology Programme*, available from The Teaching and Learning Technology Project, tel: 0117 931 7454, email: tltp@hefce.ac.uk

2 Larger student groups: developing new teaching strategies

Education A word susceptible of various definitions according to the stance of the user: eg (1) education is a passing on of a cultural heritage; (2) it is the initiation of the young into worthwhile ways of thinking and doing; (3) it is a fostering of the individual's growth. Many of the controversies in educational thought arise from the tension between these three attitudes.

Bullock, Alan and Oliver Stallybrass (eds) (1977)
The Fontana dictionary of modern thought, Fontana/Collins, London, p. 191

2.1 Pressures in teaching and learning

In higher education, we are expected to maintain the quality of our teaching of an increasing (and ever more divergent) student population without a corresponding increase in resources. At the same time, our institutions expect us to produce high-quality research.

The 'traditional' methods of university teaching and learning were established at a time when course intakes were relatively small, and based around lectures, small tutorial and seminar groups and extensive reading in pleasant, well-stocked libraries. In this system, a student could also depend on his or her tutor for personal help as a mentor. With larger student groups, however, it is proving difficult to maintain the traditional system. Many courses have well over one hundred students. The libraries cannot provide sufficient textbooks and articles – and could not house them even if they could supply them – and reading rooms are in short supply. It is increasingly difficult for tutors to be available for the needs of every student .

Figure 2.1   Some current pressures and solutions in higher education

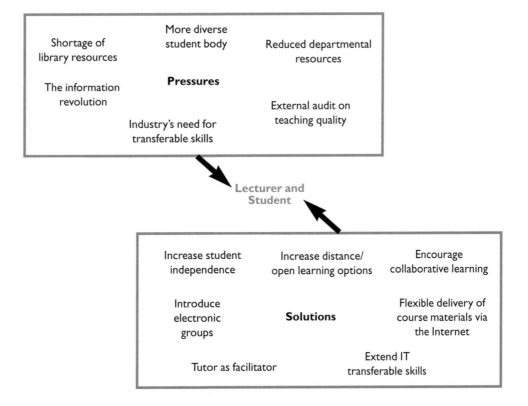

2.2 *The changing model of teaching and learning*

We are currently seeing a shift in teaching and learning models across the spectrum of higher education. This is partly in response to the increase in student numbers and external pressures from government. It is also partly in response to a growing need for graduates to emerge from university with transferable skills, such the ability to give presentations, solve problems, work independently and collaboratively as appropriate, and to use the computer as a tool, as a resource and as a means of communication.

The information revolution, our changing views on the way we teach, and demands on graduates from the workplace all work together to form a new approach to higher education. Let us start by considering some of the pressures in our daily teaching that may be forcing us to rethink our ideas.

Activity 2A **Problems you have identified in teaching larger groups**

Lectures

Seminars

Assignments

Laboratory work

Field work

● using technology in teaching and learning

For most of us the problems arise from having too many students, too few resources and too little space. Laboratory work, field work and assignments are reduced owing to lack of resources or because the marking load is too heavy. Is this scenario similar to yours?

Recent changes in education have been coupled with the introduction of new technology, and this inevitably changes methods of teaching and learning. Figure 2.2 shows some of the shifts away from traditional methods which are taking place.

Figure 2.2   *Old and new models of teaching*

Old model of teaching	New model of teaching	Technology implications
Classroom lectures	Individual exploration	Networked PCs with access to information
Passive absorption (Action/active learning)	Apprenticeship	Requires skills development and simulations
Individual work	Team learning	Benefits from collaborative tools and email
Teacher as dispenser of information	Teacher as guide	Access to experts over the network
Stable content	Fast-changing content	Requires networks and publishing tools
Homogeneity	Diversity	Requires a variety of access tools and methods

Adapted from: Byte, March 1995, p. 50

In the new teaching and learning methodology:

- the teacher becomes guide/manager of learning resources

- the student becomes more independent and manages his/her learning

- the student works collaboratively with peers, not competitively

- communication and resources are accessible via the Internet

- multimedia resources become the norm and are delivered over the network for flexible access.

Activity 2B How do you feel about your students being more independent of you?

What are your reactions to the following statements?

	Agree	Not sure	Disagree
I will lose control of my students' learning.	☐	☐	☐
Independence in learning is independence of thought.	☐	☐	☐
The quality of the course will suffer.	☐	☐	☐
It encourages students to work collaboratively.	☐	☐	☐
It is just a way to tell students to go away and get on with it.	☐	☐	☐
It will take a lot of time to set up correctly.	☐	☐	☐
It can increase the flexibility of course provision.	☐	☐	☐
It is fine, but students can't get access to books and articles needed for independent study.	☐	☐	☐
Many students will suffer if left on their own.	☐	☐	☐

Feedback *Do you see yourself as central to your students' learning and happy with teaching strategies that allow you to keep control?*

Do you see yourself as not central to your students' learning and happy with teaching strategies that give independence to your students?

Do you see yourself as someone who needs to control some aspects of your students' learning while allowing them independence at other times?

High-quality teaching is likely to involve a mixture of these approaches: there are times when tutors should remain in control and times when students will gain from independence. First, we need to be aware of the strategies we are using, and consider whether they are appropriate.

We tend to aim for more control when numbers are large, in an attempt to gain structure over such a large group; this instinct results in more work for ourselves and is not necessarily effective. Loosening control and adopting support strategies such as using teaching assistants and resource-based learning could help. Although this may mean more work initially, it will pay off in the longer term.

Using Technology   1.1   Why change how we teach in higher education?

Under the new model of learning we are moving from the tutor being a 'dispenser of information' to being a 'facilitator of learning'. Look at Figure 2.3.

Figure 2.3   Managing learning in seminars

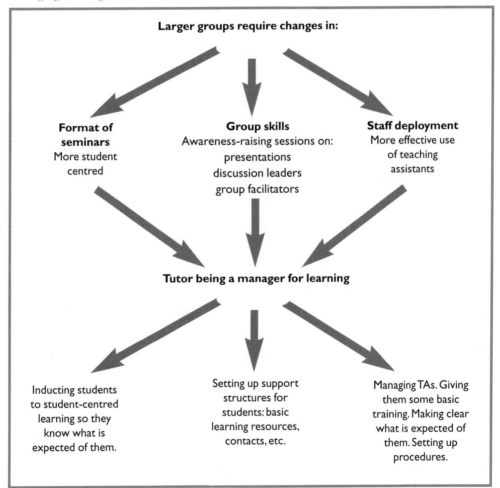

The Learning Development Services at the University of Sunderland, England, have produced open learning materials for students on student-centred learning approaches. Separate units are available.

Learning Development Services, University of Sunderland, *The effective learning programme: Unit 6 Working in groups* (1993)[1]

Gibbs (1992) *Independent learning with more students*[2]

Wade, Clowes and Houghton (1993) *Flexibility in course provision in higher education: Annual report*[3]

Martin and Darby (eds) 'Flexible and distance learning' *The CTISS File* 1994[4]

Apart from sheer size, large groups often present a more diverse student cohort, ranging from school leavers to mature students. Each group presents different challenges. The younger students have difficulty in becoming independent learners and need support to do this, while the mature group needs more flexible access to learning materials and resources to accommodate personal or work commitments, if part-time. On the other hand, mature students are generally effective independent learners.

Putting structures in place that allow for flexible access to resources and support inexperienced or weak learners to become independent learners will be the foundation of new teaching and learning methods for the year 2000 and beyond.

Gibbs, Habeshaw and Habeshaw (1992) *53 Interesting things to do in your lectures*[5]

Habeshaw, Habeshaw and Gibbs (1992) *53 Interesting things to do in your seminars and tutorials*[6]

Habeshaw, Gibbs and Habeshaw (1992) *53 Problems with large classes: making the best of a bad job*[7]

2.3   *Harnessing new technology*

Technology can be used in a wide variety of ways in education, and new forms of hardware and software offer an ever-increasing range of applications. We are not just dealing with computer-assisted learning packages, but a whole range of technology, as shown in Figure 2.4.

Figure 2.4 Uses of computers in education

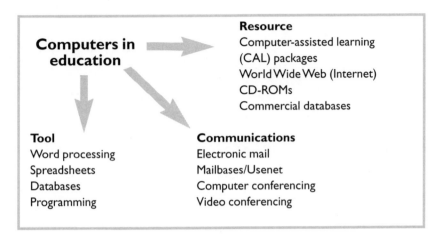

Computers in education

Resource
Computer-assisted learning (CAL) packages
World Wide Web (Internet)
CD-ROMs
Commercial databases

Tool
Word processing
Spreadsheets
Databases
Programming

Communications
Electronic mail
Mailbases/Usenet
Computer conferencing
Video conferencing

Activity 2C   How do you feel about technology?

Tick the statements that correspond most closely with your views:

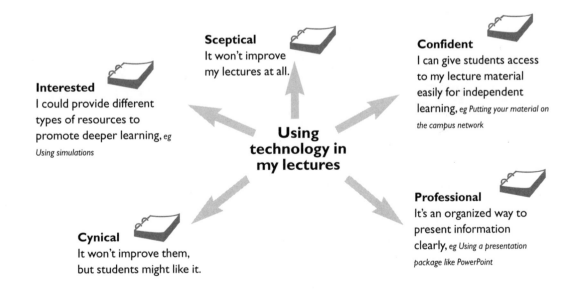

Sceptical
It won't improve my lectures at all.

Confident
I can give students access to my lecture material easily for independent learning, *eg Putting your material on the campus network*

Interested
I could provide different types of resources to promote deeper learning, *eg Using simulations*

Using technology in my lectures

Professional
It's an organized way to present information clearly, *eg Using a presentation package like PowerPoint*

Cynical
It won't improve them, but students might like it.

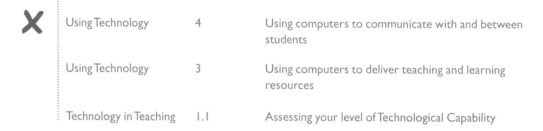

2.3.1 Using technology to make lecture material a flexible resource

Technology can provide opportunities for utilizing your lecture as a resource using:

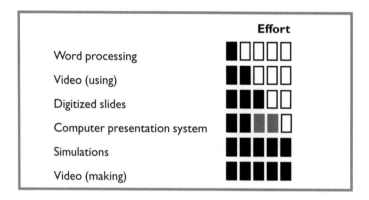

Word processing

Effort

Advantages

- A professional finish for handouts, OHP transparencies and course notes, which can be sold to students to recover costs.

- Material is easily updated and maintained.

- Different versions of documents can be stored.

Disadvantages

- You could lose your disk or your hard disk might fail (make sure you have a good back-up system).

- You'll still need to photocopy, as you will only print out a top copy.

Equipment required

- A computer with word processing software.

- A reasonably good printer, preferably a laser printer.

- OHP transparencies, if you are using OHP (you can print straight on to transparencies if you get ones suitable for your printer).

- An OHP projector to project transparencies.

Comments

From a survey carried out at Southampton University, it was found that 88% of university staff could use a word processor, a proportion which is likely to rise over time.

You need to learn to use a word processing package. If you are using a PC, choose a Windows-based package such as Microsoft Word or WordPerfect.

When producing material for OHP transparencies, a rule of thumb is that if the material is readable with the naked eye at two metres, the transparency will be legible. Large lecture theatres often need text size as large as 72 points (to be legible at the back). This by definition restricts you to summary or key points rather than long texts. As a rough guide, work with a font size of around 36 points. If you are using complicated diagrams, try to start with simple ones, building up complexity with additional overlays.

Educational implications

- Smartly laid out handouts set a standard for students' own work.

- Well laid out word-processed documents indicate professionalism towards the students as learners.

- Students are prepared to buy handouts or to download them from a server (a departmental or institutional computer where you keep your resources) and print them out as they want. This can save on secretarial time.

Video

Effort (using)

Effort (preparing/making)

Although this is not computer technology, it is being used as a medium to increase flexibility of access to course material. Video material can be digitized later and presented via the computer.

Advantages

- Dangerous or expensive experiments can be demonstrated.

- It can show equipment and procedures in preparation for expensive practicals or fieldwork.

- Additional video material can be added to illustrate a point. You will need professional help here to cut and edit your video.

- Students can access the lecture outside lecture time (flexible access), and weaker students can have the chance of repeated viewings. The video lecture becomes a learning resource available to students across the years.

- Videoing your lecture so that it replaces you physically, allowing you to use the 'the lecture hour' in an alternative way with students, for example extra seminars for small groups.

Disadvantages

- Video is an archive medium and cannot be easily changed, so it is less useful for material that will soon be out of date.

- The cost of making the video may be high (depending on complexity).

- Students may resent it replacing you. Support structures, such as scheduled contact hours, would need to be put in place for students if you used this option.

Equipment required

- If you are showing the video in a lecture theatre it needs a video player, a good screen and the facility to darken it effectively. You don't want to have to bring your own video recorder each time.

Comments

Students will need a good quality recording, so it is better to use experienced video producers. Check with your central services or other universities.

If you video your lecture in a 'studio' or laboratory you can add illustrations, or script your lectures to include video demonstrations of experiments, interviews or any other resource to give added depth.

Videoing your lecture in situ as a 'talking head' is the cheapest but not necessarily the most effective option.

Video material can be put on to a CD-ROM for easy and large-capacity storage in digital format. Once in this format it can be manipulated for any multimedia application. Check with your central services if they could do this for you.

Educational implications
- If you bring a video into the lecture, consider what its purpose is:
  - To emphasize key points?
  - To provide illustrations and examples?
  - To convey ideas visually?
  - To add variety and maintain attention?

- If you use a video to replace your lecture slot, make sure you have sufficient copies and viewing booths, otherwise viewing becomes restricted.

- A lecture can act as a meeting point with course participants and they could become disoriented if it is removed. Prepare your students for this. You may be able to replace the lecture hour with a 'clinic' to review difficult areas of the course.

| Technology in Teaching | 1.10 | Backing up your files |
| Technology in Teaching | 1.4 | What kinds of material can you put on the computer? |

Digitized slides/pictures

Effort

Slides or negatives can be digitized quite cheaply. Most high street photographic shops will provide this service. Your pictures will be placed on a CD on which you may add more pictures, to a total of approximately 100 images.

Advantages
- CD is a safe way to store a selection of slides, which can also be edited in software packages such as PhotoShop.

- You can integrate them in word-processed documents. Most word processors will allow you to incorporate pictures. (You will need a colour printer if it is important to print in full colour.)

- Adds extra visual material to your lectures.

- You can make the CD of your slides available as a learning resource.

Disadvantages
- Not suitable for material that will soon be out of date.

- Accessing your pictures over the network can be a slow business unless you have a powerful network (one with a large bandwidth). Check this with your central services.

- Resolution when projecting digitized slides can be poorer than normal slides. You need to check the degree of resolution required. This is particularly important when showing slides of X-rays, for example, where slight shade differences can indicate significant changes

Equipment required
- A multimedia PC or Mac computer.

- You will need to buy the relevant software to view the pictures. This is possible with most graphics packages, including shareware graphics packages. Ask your computing services department to help. Kodak has also produced software – ask your local photographic shop for details.

- To project the 'slides' you will need an LCD panel which is attached to the computer and the OHP. You need a powerful OHP bulb. Make sure it is at least 400 watts.

Comments
Once your slides are digitized they become available for manipulation in multimedia applications.

Educational implications
If you do bring slides into the lecture, consider what their purpose is:
– To emphasize key points?
– To provide illustrations and examples?
– To convey ideas visually?
– To add variety and maintain attention?

Technology in Teaching   1.2   Choosing a computer

Technology in Teaching   1.5   What kinds of material can you put on the computer?

Beginner's Guide to Teaching and Learning Technology[8]
http://www.icbl.hw.ac.uk/~william/cause/cause2.html

Computer presentation system

Effort

■□□□□ for text only

■■□□□ for text plus diagrams or photographs

■■■■□ if it includes multimedia

Advantages

- Allows preparation of smart/professional OHP transparencies. Most presentation packages come with 'slide' designs.

- Enables presentation of a 'slide show' via an LCD panel (or viewscreen) plugged into your computer and projected via an OHP.

- Many presentation software packages (for example, PowerPoint in Microsoft Office) are linked to a spreadsheet. They are excellent for graphs and simple simulations where you can change parameters before students' eyes.

- 'Slides' – up to six per page may be printed – as handouts for students.

- Allows you to adapt and store your material easily.

- Making slides available to students over the campus network gives flexible access to your material. Over a number of years, slides can become a learning resource.

Disadvantages

- Generally not advisable for video clips as the quality is not good enough for a large lecture theatre. Video clips usually only run in one quarter of the screen. If you enlarge the window the video movement becomes jerky. This technology is improving rapidly, so keep a check on it as very soon we shall be running video clips full-screen as a norm.

- If the quality of the LCD panel is not good, images will be poor and difficult to see. If you want to display video make sure your LCD panel can do this.

- LCD displays can be a bit of a problem in large or light lecture theatres unless limited to text or line drawings (and then at a large point size). Make sure you can darken the room sufficiently.

Equipment required

- A multimedia PC or Mac with at least 4Mb RAM (preferably at least 8 Mb for a true multimedia presentation); for a lecture theatre, a (multimedia) portable computer.

- Presentation software to prepare and display information (you will still need projection facilities like an LCD panel and OHP). PowerPoint in Microsoft Office is an example of such software.

- An LCD panel (or equivalent) to project the 'slides' you prepare in the package. You may be able to borrow one from a central services department.

- An OHP with at least a 400 watt bulb if using an LCD panel. LCD panels projected via an OHP tend to be dark, so you need as bright a bulb as possible. Check the brightness in the room beforehand if you can.

Comments

If you are going to use multimedia you will need access to services to digitize sound, video and slides. Multimedia computers allow the capture of sound through speaking directly into a microphone which is plugged into the computer. The quality may not be good enough, however, for large group presentations.

Keep your presentation clear and simple. Projection in a large lecture theatre reduces clarity.

Check with your central services department what they are able to offer you. Also find out how well equipped your lecture theatres are for computer presentations of any kind.

Educational implications

- If you produce a multimedia presentation, ask yourself the purpose of the additional media:
    - To emphasize key points?
    - To provide illustrations and examples?
    - To convey ideas visually?
    - To add variety and maintain attention?

- Professional-looking OHP slides indicate professionalism on the course and give students standards to aim for. Why not encourage student seminar leaders to use the same technology?

- Making lecture notes/presentations available over the computer network allows for flexible access to your material.

Warren (1993) *Understanding IT: computer-based presentations*[9]

Technology in Teaching	1.2	Choosing a computer
Technology in Teaching	1.6	Presenting your information in a lecture theatre
Technology in Teaching	1.8	Making a presentation using a computer

Simulations

Effort

or, if you can already program:

Advantages
- Useful for demonstrating standard processes, models, systems and difficult concepts.

- Allows students to interact with the simulation outside the lecture, if it is made available. This becomes a course resource, increases access and is ideal for weaker students who may need repeated viewings.

- The simulation becomes a learning resource available to students across the years.

Disadvantages
- Some programming skills are needed to get a simulation working. This depends on the software you are using. Spreadsheets, for example, can demonstrate simple simulation with an intermediate understanding of the spreadsheet.

- You could buy an authoring package that allows you to produce simulations, but you need to invest in learning the program.

Equipment required
- PC or Mac.

- A suitable piece of software to produce a simulation. This can range from authoring type programs like Macromind Director, to programming in Visual Basic or to spreadsheets.

- You need to project your simulation if presenting to a group. This can be done via an LCD panel connected to your computer and an OHP.

- A network or stand-alone computers so that students may access the simulation.

Comments

Simulations help students to understand how systems and models work. A simulation can be regarded as a learning resource and possibly added to computer-assisted learning packages. You could make your simulations available to students across the network. Check with your computer services if they have any particular regulations for doing this. In lectures, when you are using your simulations make sure they are clearly presented and visible for large groups and those sitting at the back.

Spreadsheets with small highlighted cells may not be helpful, and graphical forms may be more readily understood. The simpler the lines, the easier they are to see from a distance. Select text size (36 points or larger) and graphical lines suitable for large lecture theatres.

Educational implications

- This is a very useful didactic strategy for conveying difficult ideas.

- Can be used to prepare students for laboratory work where complex processes are at work, but not visible.

- Best when used as a course resource so students can experiment with the model.

- Depending on the simulation, students may able to test their ideas within the model, gaining a deeper understanding of a complex area.

Technology in Teaching   1.4   What kinds of material can you put on the computer?

Cuttle, Young and Heath (1993) *A practical introduction to creating courseware with Microsoft Excel*[10]

2.3.2   *Lecture aids as a learning resource*

Wherever possible, you should be looking at making your lecture aids a course resource for students. This may mean that students won't turn up to lectures, but if you move towards being a 'facilitator of learning' this may not be such a bad thing. Make sure your resources are equally available to all, with as much flexible access as possible. Access can be achieved via:

- stand-alone computers in your department – make sure there are enough computers
- networking, either on your departmental network or the campus-wide network. Make sure you have complied with the necessary regulations allowing you to put

material on the network. Check with your computing services department well in advance

– the Internet via the World Wide Web. Make sure there are enough computers available with World Wide Web browsers such as Mosaic or Netscape. Check whether your university/faculty has a World Wide Web page you can link from. Will anyone be able to do this for you?

With such methods you can cater for larger groups. Your next concern, however, is providing support mechanisms for students and remaining in contact, through designated 'clinic' sessions, your teaching assistants or electronic mail.

2.4 Assessing large groups

As institutions move towards a more modular approach to study, there is an increasing need to develop a coherent assessment system across the institution as well as evaluating how we assess our students. This includes the use of technology.

Figure 2.5   Issues in assessment

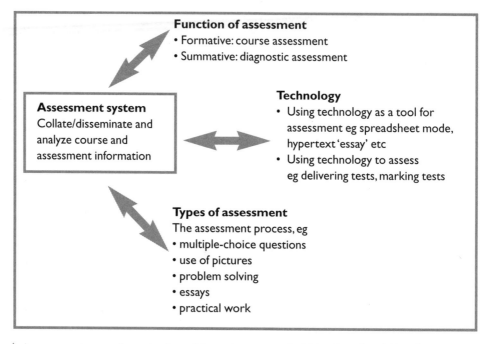

Function of assessment
- Formative: course assessment
- Summative: diagnostic assessment

Assessment system
Collate/disseminate and analyze course and assessment information

Technology
- Using technology as a tool for assessment eg spreadsheet mode, hypertext 'essay' etc
- Using technology to assess eg delivering tests, marking tests

Types of assessment
The assessment process, eg
- multiple-choice questions
- use of pictures
- problem solving
- essays
- practical work

Assessment procedures and marking schemes are held by the school/faculty or department. This information is held in various formats across disciplines, and at present it is quite difficult to analyse this data fully. Having an assessment system for collecting such information could help.

Apart from computerizing examination marks, an overall system could also give accurate and full information to students on the content of their study, allowing them to make informed decisions about the course they want to take. Such information should also be sufficiently complete to help external examiners check that the assessment process adequately reflects the content of the course. However, when collecting such information on students, you have to make sure you are observing data protection legislation. You need to understand fully the implications of this legislation before implementing any computerized system

Activity 2D Your view of the assessment procedure at your institution

- What external mechanisms are there for drawing attention to errors and discrepancies in marking?

- Are you satisfied that they are as good as they could be?

- Is the mechanism effective? Can you give examples?

- Do you consider that every faculty/school/department should have the right to aggregate and process students' marks as it wishes?

- Medical grounds apart, justify your right to amend students' marks at examinations boards.

- Do you feel competent to judge and quantify the effect of illness on a student's examination performance?

- Would your examinations boards' decisions be fairer if all marks were considered anonymously?

- Would you wish to have any more data on students' performance available at examinations boards? If so, what?

- If more data would help, why are you not receiving it already?

- Should it be any concern of your institution centrally whom you appoint as external examiner? In what way or ways?

Source: Partington (1993) p. 16

Partington (1993) *Quality and information technology in assessment procedures*[11]

2.4.1 Different functions of assessment

Broadly speaking, assessment can be broken down into two areas: formative assessment and summative assessment.

Formative assessment
This refers to 'testing' that can help students with their learning. It is a way of pinpointing weak points across a whole class or within individual students. These assessments can be taken by students alone as self-assessment exercises in a very informal way or in a more formal way with the tutor.

Summative assessment
This refers to the 'end of course' assessment. Assessment procedures here are more rigorous and the student is given a grade which contributes to his or her final degree or acts as a 'pass' or 'fail' on a particular course.

The summative assessment procedures are generally laid down at school/faculty or departmental level. These procedures tend to be less creative and fall under the scrutiny of quality assessors. Formative assessment, on the other hand, allows you and your students to build into the learning process a series of assessments that could help them creatively with their learning.

Peer or collaborative assessment

Peer or collaborative assessment is one method that could be experimented with at the formative level. This approach to assessment presupposes that students are working within a collaborative learning environment, be this face-to-face, on-line or a mixture of the two. They have built up a *modus operandi* of working together collaboratively and should therefore not feel threatened by collaborative assessment.

According to David McConnell (1995) it is necessary to draw up guidelines for collaborative assessment, and these might include:

- the assessment to be a learning process in itself
- a separation of grade from discussion feedback
- the discussion to focus on the learning that has taken place as a result of the assignment and its meaning to the individual concerned
- discussion points such as:
    - What led you to choose the assignment topic?
    - What were you trying to do in the assignment?
    - How do you feel it went – both the process and the product?
    - Would you approach the topic in a different way if you were to start afresh?
    - How satisfied are you with what you have done?
- a minimum group size: the learner, a peer and a tutor. Larger groups of four or six can also be effective.

In order to do this effectively, students, tutors or both groups need to determine beforehand the criteria for judging such work. By using collaborative and peer assessment, your students will gain from being able to evaluate and discuss the work of others and critically view their own work for both the process and the product. The value of this for their learning is far superior to that of just gaining a score on a piece of work.

McConnell (1995) *Implementing computer-supported co-operative learning*[12]

Boud (1987) *Implementing student self assessment*[13]

Falchikov (1993) *Group process analysis: self and peer assessment of working together in a group*[14]

Debate on Skywriting
   http://cogsci.soton.ac.uk/~harnad

Political Science Discourse Journal (on-line unrefereed journal used for peer review)
   http://www.soton.ac.uk/~psd

2.4.2 Some uses of technology in assessment

Technology is predominantly used in formative assessment and provides an excellent way to aid student learning, giving key feedback when it is needed without resorting to the tutor. A technological solution to assessment has many advantages over its paper counterpart:
- it allows more than one attempt
- it can supply hints or a 'cheat' key
- it can give immediate feedback
- it can guide students' reading as a result of the test
- you can feed in distracters to students as they progress
- useful for formative or summative assessment
- if summative, it will allow only one attempt (as with paper)
- standard tests or random test questions can be given.

Technology can be used in assessment in a variety of ways:
- to collate, disseminate and analyse course and assessment data
- as a tool of assessment
- to assess learning.

Technology to collate, disseminate and analyse course and assessment data
In section 2.4 we touched briefly on the value of having a comprehensive computerized system for assessment purposes. Preferably this system would need to be designed by some central section using professional systems analysts.

Technology as a tool of assessment
Increasingly, departments are asking students to produce a piece of assessed work using technology. This can include:
- word-processed essays
- hypermedia information systems devised by, for example, archaeology and history students (often for display in museums)
- computer-based training packages on areas of their own discipline (these are like hypermedia essays)
- computer-aided designs by engineering students
- spreadsheet modelling for a wide variety of disciplines
- presentations using packages like PowerPoint.

Using Technology	3	Using computers to deliver teaching and learning resources, section 3.4.1
Technology in Teaching	5.6	Using the World Wide Web section
Using Technology	2.3	Harnessing new technology

In addition to academic content, these activities can also be seen as contributing to valuable transferable skills.

Technology to assess learning

Technology can also be used to prepare, deliver and mark assessment questions.

Various pieces of software can be used to prepare tests and quizzes, including authoring programs such as Toolbook, Guide and Authorware. These packages can offer text or full hypermedia facilities when producing tests. The World Wide Web is also being used as a delivery, marking and submission medium.

The use of authoring programs for assessment usually occurs because the course material itself is presented as a computer-aided learning package. Building in quizzes and self-assessment exercises is a natural extension. Hypertext can build up a system of elaborate feedback for students, directing them to parts of the package that can help them. It can also deal with questions that have no right or wrong answers, using the students' selection to discuss the pros and cons of choosing that answer. This is good for building on more complex knowledge.

Case Study 1

Assessment in pharmaceutical biology using Authorware:
University of Brighton

The Pharmacy Consortium for Computer Aided Learning (PCCAL) has developed a series of tutorials for student self-assessment using the authoring package Authorware. They have developed five 20-minute modules containing a series of questions. These questions involve clicking areas on diagrams, text entry, click-drag and push-button activities. The presentation and position of questions has been randomized so that students will not receive the same questions at the same time. Students are presented with a score at the end of the session and a feedback button to give them more in-depth explanations of answers and point them to further reading. Tutors use these scores to identify students whose performance is weak, offering further help. The aim of the assessment modules is to give students an opportunity to assess, revise and reinforce their basic knowledge in this area.

Contact: Dr Andrew Lloyd, Department of Pharmacy, University of Brighton, Moulescomb, Brighton BN2 4GJ, England
Tel. 01273 642049, *email: AWL1 @bton.ac.uk*

Case Study 2

Assessing students on a software engineering course via the World Wide Web: University of Sunderland

The assessment procedure is for a course on software engineering for computing and non-computing students. All material for the course is presented on the Internet via the World Wide Web. The exercises and answer forms are embedded in the teaching material. Many of the questions are based on multiple choice (MCQs). Lecturers can create their assessment questions from a database. Once the assessment has been completed, the system automatically marks the MCQs and the results are sent to the lecturer (arriving at his/her email address) and the student. The lecturer can then forward these marks to the administration system quite easily.

Contact: Ian Ferguson, School of Computing and Information Systems, Priestman Building, Green Terrace, Sunderland, Tyne & Wear SR1 3SD, England
Tel: 0191 515 2508
Email: ian.ferguson@sunderland.ac.uk

Case Study 3

Formative and summative assessment on a physics CAL package: University of Surrey

The TLTP consortium, SToMP (student teaching of modular physics) uses both formative and summative techniques in the CAL package. Their formative assessment is in-line questions with easily accessible answers in a pop-up window or at the end of a link. They also have a purpose-built testing utility based on MCQs, pair matching, rank ordering or numeric style answers. These questions appear in one window with another window accepting the answers. Built into this formative model is assistance and directed feedback. The summative mode will allow students only one attempt at each question. The questions and marking scheme are under the control of academic staff.

Contact: Dick Bacon, Department of Physics, University of Surrey, Guildford GU2 5XH, England
Tel: 01483 509414 *Email: phsldb@ph.surrey.ac.uk*

In addition to hypermedia authoring packages to create assessments, there is also purpose-built software. Such a commercial product is Question Mark. It is available for DOS, Windows and the Macintosh. There is also a utility that allows you to convert Question Mark files for use on the World Wide Web (QM Web). The software is ideal for producing summative assessments as there is full text encryption, which prevents students breaking in to see questions and answers. It can support question types such as:

– multiple-choice (MCQ) with True/False, Yes/No, Agree/Disagree
– multiple response
– explanation
– push-button multiple-choice
– graphical hotspot
– text questions.

A demo disk is available from Question Mark, 41b Brecknock Road, London N7 0BT, England Tel: 0171 263 7575, World Wide Web site: *http://www.qmark.com/*

Examine is purpose-built software developed by Tim Brailsford at the University of Nottingham. It is available for PC and they are working on a Mac version. It is not as secure as Question Mark, as there is no encryption. It would therefore be primarily suitable for formative assessment. The question types it can handle are:

– multiple-choice (2–6 possible answers)
– more than one correct answer
– numeric (positive or negative numbers – not scientific notation)
– text (up to 150 words – although these are not computer assessed).

Students receive a score at the end with a list of their questions answered correctly (plus the text answers).

It is available (at £25.00) from UCoSDA; for a catalogue, email: *ucosda@sheffield.ac.uk*

Finally, computer technology can be used to mark assessments using an optical mark reader (OMR). The test needs to be prepared on special paper necessary for the OMR software. The answers from multiple-choice questions are scanned into the computer and the software reads and totals the scores. This method has proved difficult to use. If you are interested, see Terry King's article

King *Using an optical mark reader for continuous student assessment: a case study in higher education.*[15]

2.4.3 *Writing assessments*

Formative and summative assessments indicate the level of formality of testing, whether it's diagnostic or towards the final award. However, the kind of assessment you finally choose depends on another dichotomy: product assessment and/or performance assessment (Rowntree (1994) p. 153). For assessment to be successful and reflect what is learned on the course, you need to decide if you are measuring a product or a process.

Product assessment

This refers to a physical product that is assessed such as essays, reports, multiple-choice questions, calculations, drawings, engineering products or architectural plans.

Performance assessment

This refers to an activity or the process of making the product. This kind of testing is needed if you want to know how learners do or make something.

In some cases, however, you may well be measuring both a product and a process. This is particularly useful in peer assessment where performance aspects can be left to the group and the product to the tutor.

Types of questions and exercises

Once you have decided if you are going to use product or process style of assessment, you will then need to decide on the format the test will take.

Figure 2.6   *Open and closed questions*

Closed questions	Open questions	
multiple-choice questions multiple gap fill gap fill drag and drop (labelling pictures) rank order hotspot pictures matching	problem solving plans essays practicals drawings	**Product**
	decision making practicals interviewing problem solving	**Process**

Adapted from Rowntree (1994)[16]

Closed questions: product

This is the largest and most developed category and the one most favoured by computer-aided assessment. Use these types of tests if you want your learners to distinguish between a set of possible answers. This kind of assessment is usually used as quizzes in formative assessment.

Feedback with such questions is very important as the learning experience from this kind of testing can be virtually nil if there is little or no feedback (see feedback section below).

Open questions: product

These are more expansive assessment procedures and can offer students a quality learning experience. The focus for the student is planning, researching the topic, and bringing it to fruition. You will need to use this kind of test if you want your students to define, explain, justify, invent or produce something. In this category the assessment procedure is looking at the outcome or product and not the process of 'getting there'.

Open questions: process

This is a similar group of testing devices as above, but here you are looking at the process of the product, as much as (if not more than) the product itself. If you want to know how your students worked, interacted and thought through an assessment, then use this approach.

Assessment feedback

One of the major complaints with summative assessment is that the students get very little feedback. As lecturers we know this can be very difficult to change and you may even have rules at your institutions forbidding you from giving individual exam marks. We should therefore make sure that when we use formative assessment our feedback is as rich and creative as possible, and actually enhances the learning process. Some of the possibilities are shown below.

Figure 2.7   Possibilities for assessment feedback

Type of feedback	Comment
A score or no score	Scoring can be useful if accompanied by more constructive feedback on the answers. On its own it adds little to the learning process.
A pop-up window with the correct answer	This kind of feedback is usual in hypertext/hypermedia software as well as assessment software. It usually only gives the correct answer. Some extra information saying why an answer is right or wrong would help.
Suggest an answer	Sometimes there may be several answers. Either list all possibilities or state what you think is the best fit and say why.
If 'wrong' what to do? If 'right' what to do?	Giving scores and the correct answer are the most common way of dealing with right and wrong answers. However, if you are using hypertext/hypermedia you could expand this. If the answer is 'wrong', point students to relevant literature. If 'correct', point them to further reading or related topics.
Computer noises as feedback	These tend to be used for light-hearted quizzes and are not a good idea for serious work. Other students in the computer room would soon recognize those students who made lots of mistakes.
Comments to students	Avoid patronizing feedback. Keep to the content rather than commenting on the student. However, if you used a scoring system, you may wish to give constructive feedback to students below a certain level.

Submitting the answers

You may not want your students to submit their answers, especially if testing is self-assessment. However, if you do wish to keep track of your students' progress, here are some methods:

- Via email. This is particularly useful if you've got assessment questions on World Wide Web pages. Students' answers can be immediately sent to the lecturer's email address or some other specified address.
- Saving answers to a local hard disk or the server. If students save to a local hard disk then you will have to go around to every machine to access the information. If they have saved it on a central server, it is easier for you to access. Make sure students are familiar with how to save their test.

– Submit the test on a floppy disk. If students are able to write to any machine, you could ask them to save it on a floppy. Collecting and processing such information could be time consuming.

– Submit answers on paper. Questions could appear on the screen for students to select. This would be suitable for more open-ended questions where feedback would be difficult on the computer.

Whatever form of assessment we use, we must make sure our students know how and why they are being assessed.

Technology in Teaching   5.6   Learning to create Web pages using HTML

Brown and Pendelbury (1992) *Assessing active learning*[17]

Gibbs, Habeshaw and Habeshaw (1988) *53 Interesting ways to assess your students*[18]

Rowntree (1994) *Preparing materials for open, distance and flexible learning*[16]

Computer Assisted Assessment
  http://medweb.bham.ac.uk/http/caa/caa.html
This is a searchable MCQ database from the University of Birmingham. Some of the items on this Web site are:

– Make your own custom test!
– Working questions already posted by others
– Demonstration of the system using dummy questions
– Password protected demo (enter username 'caa', password 'beta')
– A list of question templates for submitting your own questions
– Documentation for posting your own questions.

Delivery of question sets over WWW
  http://www.ets.bris.ac.uk/ets/resource/tutorial/tutorial.htm

Example from the tutorial web page

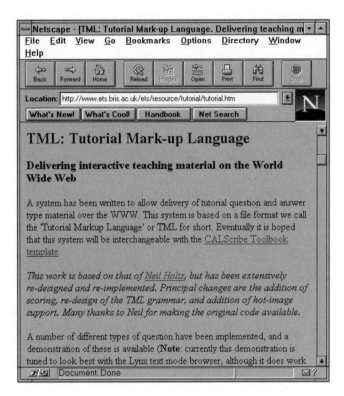

References for Chapter 2

[1] Learning Development Services, University of Sunderland, *The effective learning programme: Unit 6 – Working in groups* (1993), University of Sunderland, Langham Tower, Ryhope Road, Sunderland SR2 7EE, England

[2] Gibbs, Graham (1992), *Independent learning with more students*, Polytechnics and Colleges Funding Council
This is a booklet in a series from the Teaching More Students Project. Other titles are:
　　　　1 Problems and course design strategies
　　　　2 Lecturing to more students
　　　　3 Discussion with more students
　　　　4 Assessing more students
Further information from the Oxford Centre for Staff Development, tel: 01865 819172

[3] Wade, Winnie, Susan Clowes and Jim Houghton (1993), *Flexibility in course provision in higher education: Annual report*, Flexible Learning Initiative, Loughborough University
This report is a series of case studies on projects implementing flexible course provision.

[4] Martin, Joyce and Jonathan Darby (eds), 'Flexible and distance learning' in *The CTISS File*, 17 July 1994
A series of articles from various university practitioners.
For more information on CTISS (now called Active Learning), contact Jonathan Darby or Joyce Martin, tel: 01865 273273 or email: CTISS@vax.ox.ac.uk

[5] Gibbs, Graham, Sue Habeshaw and Trevor Habeshaw (1992), *53 Interesting things to do in your lectures*, Technical and Educational Services Ltd, 37 Ravenswood Road, Bristol BS6 6BW, England

[6] Habeshaw, Sue, Trevor Habeshaw and Graham Gibbs (1992), *53 Interesting things to do in your seminars and tutorials*, Technical and Educational Services Ltd, 37 Ravenswood Road, Bristol BS6 6BW, England

[7] Habeshaw, Sue, Graham Gibbs and Trevor Habeshaw (1992), *53 Problems with large classes: making the best of a bad job*, Technical and Educational Services Ltd, 37 Ravenswood Road, Bristol BS6 6BW, England

[8] *Beginner's guide to Teaching and Learning Technology:*
Hard copy available from UCoSDA, tel: 0114 272 5248 or email: *ucosda@sheffield.ac.uk*

[9] Warren, Lorraine (1993), *Understanding IT: computer-based presentations*, CVCP/USDU, Sheffield
For a copy, contact UCoSDA, tel: 0114 272 5248 or email: *ucosda@sheffield.ac.uk*

[10] Cuttle, Mary, Clive P. Young and Simon Heath (1993), *A practical introduction to creating courseware with Microsoft Excel*, CTI Centre for Land Use and Environmental Sciences
To request a copy, tel: 01224 480291 or email: *CTILand@aberdeen.ac.uk*

[11] Partington, John (1993), *Quality and information technology in assessment procedures*, Occasional Green Paper 5, UCoSDA, Sheffield, England. Enquiries to UCoSDA, tel: 0114 272 5248 or email: *ucosda@sheffield.ac.uk*

[12] McConnell, David (1995), *Implementing computer-supported co-operative learning*, Kogan Page, London

[13] Boud, David (1987), *Implementing student self-assessment*, Sydney: HERSDA

[14] Falchikov, Nancy, 'Group process analysis: self and peer assessment of working together in a group' in *Educational & Training Technology International*, 30 (3), August 1993, pp. 275–283
The process of working together was assessed by the group while the product of the exercise was assessed by the lecturer. The choice of project was devolved to group members.

[15] King, Terry, 'Using an optical mark reader for continuous student assessment: a case study in higher education' in Jonathon Darby & Joyce Martin (eds) 'Computer-assisted assessment' in *Active Learning* (1), December 1994, pp. 23–25

[16] Rowntree, Derek (1994), *Preparing materials for open, distance and flexible learning: an action guide for teachers and trainers*, Kogan Page, London

[17] Brown, G.A. and M. Pendelbury (1992), *Assessing active learning*, Sheffield, UCoSDA
This book gives guidance on writing multiple-choice questions.

[18] Gibbs Graham, Sue Habeshaw and Trevor Habeshaw (1988), *53 Interesting ways to assess your students*, Technical and Educational Services Ltd, 37 Ravenswood Road, Bristol BS6 6BW, England

3 Using computers to deliver teaching and learning resources

What general advantages can technology-based teaching and learning be expected to offer? This section outlines three main advantages: (1) the ability to deliver a complete course which the student sees from beginning to end; (2) the ability to simulate real-life processes, such as dangerous experiments and complex procedures, view them and experiment with them; (3) the opportunity to create elaborate graphical representations which can be developed and explored interactively by students.

3.1 Computer-delivered resources

In education, computers are often associated with computer-assisted learning packages that are generally delivered in a stand-alone mode in open learning or resource-based learning centres. The educational community is beginning to see a wider use for computers in teaching and learning: as a delivery medium for resources; as a communication medium for collaborative learning; and as a tool, using traditional software packages.

This section looks at computers as a delivery medium for resources.

Figure 3.1

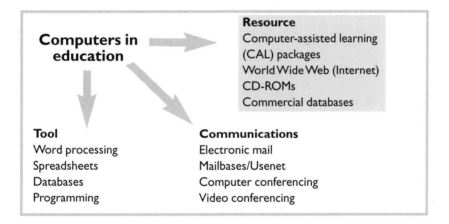

3.2 Why consider more flexible teaching and learning patterns?

Computers offer great flexibility in the type of resource we can present to students (multimedia resources especially) as well as increasing flexibility of access to information.

Greater flexibility in education is one strategy for dealing with the increased numbers and diversity of students. It is a strategy that is essentially looking at alternative ways of presenting material to students and allowing them to learn where and when it best suits them. It is also a strategy which develops independent and collaborative learning. Such a strategy could mean increased availability to key resources (longer opening times for the library, for example, and more access to computing facilities). Many universities already operate a 9am–10pm day.

As lecturers we can take advantage of this by providing independent learning materials (open learning) in central locations like the library, and making some of our material available on computer, over the campus network. If we decide to do this, then we need to start thinking about how we can write learning packages (whether for the computer or for print) that relieve us of repetitive teaching activities.

A wide variety of terminology is used to cover the area of independent learning, with a great deal of conceptual overlap (see Figure 3.2).

Figure 3.2   Common ways to support independent learning

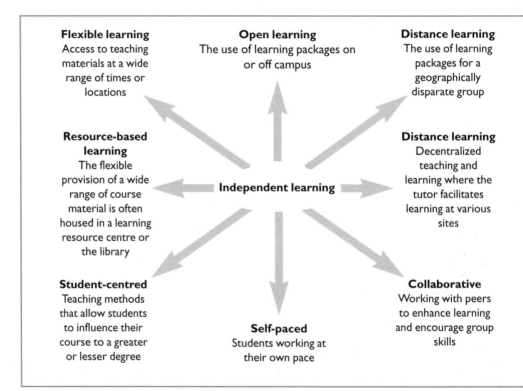

Open and distance education are no longer restricted to UK institutions like the Open University, the Open College or company training schemes. It is becoming an ever-increasing part of traditional universities and other higher education establishments as already in the US and Australia. Many further education colleges and newer universities have invested in various models of independant learning as a strategy for delivering a wide range of teaching and learning material.

Open University Homepage (UK)
http://www.open.ac.uk/

The Open University Homepage (US)
http://www.open.com/

Extramural Open University Study (New Zealand)
http://www.massey.ac.nz/~wwcues

Open Learning Australia
http://www.ola.edu.au/whatis.htm

International Centre for Distance Learning (ICDL)
A comprehensive website from the Open University in the UK on issues in distance learning
http://www-icdl.open.ac.uk

International Centre for Distance Learning (ICDL)
A sample of international open/distance education universities
http://www-icdl.open.ac.uk/info/desources.htm

3.3   *Learning packs: some basic principles*

Traditionally, learning packs have been associated with good quality distance learning institutions like the Open University or, of late, low-level qualifications. This is now changing as independent learning becomes a fact of life for our students.

For most of us this will mean completely rethinking how we teach our subject and will be a very time consuming and thought provoking process. If we are interested, we need to decide which parts of a course are best served by this method and then whether it is advisable to buy in open learning material, work alone on writing the pack, work in a team or collaborate with an 'external' team of course writers.

Learning packs are traditionally seen as readers with exercises or assignments, as in the early Open University model. There are, however, more structured packs based on pedagogical principles of reader interactivity, as well as optimal page layouts for learning material. In addition to print, many packs also include video, audio, television and radio; foreign language courses are a classic example of this.

Computer technology is now playing a vital role in this field of education. We can use computers to prepare and deliver teaching and learning resources, and as a medium for communicating between lecturers and students.

Beginner's Guide to Teaching and Learning Technology
http://www.icbl.hw.ac.uk/~william/cause/cause2.html

3.3.1 *Using learning packs to support lecture-based courses*

Learning packs are more than just handouts, but they need not necessarily be complex. We are already using some intermediary learning packs, as shown in Figure 3.3.

Figure 3.3   Learning packs which support lecture-based courses

Learning Pack	Description	Advantages
Lecture Packages	Full student notes with exercises/problems that students need to be familiar with *before* the lecture. It is better if they are given the whole set before the lecture.	Lectures can focus on problem areas, additional material and overviews. It may even be possible to dispense with lecture sessions.
Readers/Study Guides	Core textual material which is difficult to obtain, eg chapters from books and articles. These may be accompanied by commentaries, questions, summaries and seminar topics as well as further reading lists.	Ensure that everyone has access to key texts and all students can be prepared for seminars. They also structure the topic, giving students a framework for their own research.
Laboratory/Field Journals	A short description of each 'activity' (experiment/field work) with information on: • instructions to carry it out • analysis methods • relation to theory • report writing techniques • reading lists. See also manuals/guides.	Students may be able to carry out their work without an academic member of staff being there, with technical staff providing the equipment needed.
Manuals and Guides	Used for equipment, instruments, computer-based learning packages, project work, dissertations, safety regulations.	Equipment and instrument manuals could be held at suitable access points for use when necessary.
Course Guides	These contain: • course aims/rationale • timetable • learning contract • key texts • commentaries • seminar titles/expected • performance • methods of assessment • assignments • additional media such as computers, audio, video • reading lists.	These prepare the student for the breadth of the course. He/she is aware of what is expected from day one. Many non-essential face-to-face sessions can be dispensed with.

Source: Gibbs 'Designing learning packages: Module 8' in *Certificate in Teaching in Higher Education by Open Learning*[1]

Activity 3A What material do you use in support of a lecture course?

	Regularly	Sometimes	Never
Course guides			
Lecture notes (handed out each week)			
Lecture packages			
Readers/study guides			
Reading lists			
Problem/exercise sheets			
Laboratory/field journals			
Instructions for coursework, laboratory, field work (handed out each week)			
Manuals and guides			
This material is word-processed			

If you have answered 'yes' to most of these and if they have been word-processed, you are well on your way to producing a full-blown learning package. The effort needed to move to more independent learning material is therefore reduced.

Figure 3.4   Issues to consider before writing a learning pack

Element	Issues	Possible IT solutions	Considerations
Student body	Your student body is heterogeneous in terms of age, past experience, cultural background and ability	Increased access to core learning materials and exercises via print and computer-assisted learning (CAL) materials	Students need sufficient computers to access the material without too much difficulty; public learning environments need to be created
Volume of information	Your subject has a high volume of facts and figures to disseminate	Use a variety of resources from packs to primary sources (a resource-based learning approach) Use a mixture of electronic and paper-based resources	Such resources need to be 'signposted' well for students You will need to assess students' computer literacy; they probably need basic training to get them going See 'Student body' above
Group work	Your course (or part of it) involves students working together solving problems, dealing with case studies, etc	You could encourage or expect use of computers to help solve problems, eg spreadsheets, databases, word processors, graphics packages Could your group work be achieved at a distance using electronic communications? You could use an electronic environment to display the best of students' work; the idea could be developed for peer evaluation	See 'Student body' above Students need an account and email ID; check with your computer services. What about training? This needs to be cleared with students first
Staff time	You need to reduce your face-to-face teaching time	Increase independent learning using print and electronic learning packs Encourage email discussion of certain topics	There is an initial high cost in time and equipment to start: make sure your student numbers are high and that you teach the course often enough

3.3.2 Key considerations when writing learning packs

We are not going to go into detail here about how to write learning packs. We will simply point to key areas and suggest some further reading. These suggestions apply to both paper-based and computer-based learning packages.

● Know your learner. Are there any consistent misconceptions about your topic that you could address?

● Make the nature and structure of your pack clear: lead in learners, set objectives, include 'maps', advanced organizers, and case studies to illustrate application, and give summaries and overviews.

● Make your pack as interactive as possible by including:
– self-assessed questions
– multiple-choice questions
– true/false statements
– gap-filling exercises
– ordering tasks
– rank order exercises
– decision-making using a case-based approach
– open-ended tasks (essays, commentaries, summaries, flow charts, diagrams).

Also consider how you will respond to learner responses (key activities should be tutor assessed):
– include feedback within the pack
– provide tutor-assessed work
– consider computer-marked work
– present activities clearly
– avoid trivial exercises
– vary activities.

● Add visual material, leave lots of white space, box texts for emphasis or asides, and chunk texts. Take photographs, and make tape recordings where appropriate.

● Plan learner support, feedback and tutor-marked assignments into the programme.

Race (1992) *53 Interesting ways to write open learning materials*[2]

Rowntree (1994) *Preparing materials for open, distance and flexible learning*[3]

3.4 How computer technology can increase flexible access to learning resources

Computer technology allows us to present a wide range of multimedia resources that have been made accessible to the computer through a process known as digitization. If I digitize clips from video, for example, I am converting it to computer-readable format. Most traditional forms of teaching and learning resources from all media can be digitized:

Texts

These can be digitized with a scanner. It may be necessary to keep handwritten texts as archive material. In this case the text will be scanned as if it were a picture, so you won't be able to edit it.

You can scan text in as text and then edit it. You will need software known as optical character recognition so that it can be transferred to a word processing program.

Pictures and line drawings

Scanners can be used to digitize the images which can then be 'touched up' using software such as Adobe PhotoShop and Jasc PaintShop Pro.

You can also 'grab' single images from a digitized video and save it in a picture format (eg as a bitmap) and manipulate them in paint packages.

Slides stored on CD-ROM

You can take your slides to a photographic store and have them developed and stored on a CD-ROM. A CD-ROM can hold 650Mb of information. A standard enlarged print takes approximately 1.5Mb. A CD-ROM could hold 100 slides.

Digitizing video clips

Through additional hardware in your computer, you can digitize 'normal' (analogue) video. It needs a lot of storage space, so use it wisely and effectively. One minute of video (compressed in order to minimize the storage space required) takes up approximately 12Mb.

Digitizing sound

Multimedia PCs and the Mac have the ability to record and play back sound. As with video, sound files are large and should be used wisely. One minute of sound occupies approximately 9Mb.

Educational implications

Once we have digitized our resources, we can integrate them more easily. To obtain full educational benefit from them, we must use them discriminately. Some issues for consideration are outlined below.

Video and images

What is the educational function of the video? What can it bring to your materials that text alone cannot do? Choose video clips that add information and are not merely

there for 'light relief'. Video can be used effectively to:
- show how equipment works
- show how procedures and processes function
- show interactive strategies: body movement, gestures, etc
- illustrate complex models.

Whenever you feel you need a whole page to describe something that can be shown effectively by a one- or two-minute video clip, use the video clip.

If you don't have video, some of these items can be replaced by pictures, graphics or simulations, particularly if the illustration does not need to contain transformation or movement.

Sound

What is the educational function of a piece of sound you want to include? What can it bring to your materials that text alone cannot do? Some examples that benefit from sound are:
- courting noises of various animals
- pronunciation in language learning
- hearing examples of various languages
- other animal noises that relate to your text
- music in general, and instruments in particular
- error identification of equipment through sound
- sounds that are generally below or beyond our hearing threshold.

There are many reasons for adding sound, but its educational function must be recognized.

Beginner's Guide to Teaching and Learning Technology
 http://www.icbl.hw.ac.uk/~william/cause/cause2.html

Once our material is digitized and we know its educational function, we can use it in the following ways:
- as a basis for resource-based learning *
- for use in authoring packages such as Toolbook, if we want to produce our own computer learning package
- as stand-alone items, such as slides
- to add sound to a wordprocessing file
- to add video to a lecture presentation through software packages such as Microsoft PowerPoint**

* Technology in Teaching   1.4.4   Audio

**Technology in Teaching   1.8   Making a presentation using a computer

These resources can then be delivered either in a stand-alone situation on one computer in a resource centre, or made available across the campus using a campus-wide network. You will need to talk to someone in your computing services department (or equivalent) on how to do this.

If you do decide to deliver your resources across the campus network, check the availability of computers with your central services.

Warren (1993) *Understanding IT: computer-based presentations*[4]

3.4.1 *Some examples of computer-delivered resources*

This section looks at the following ways in which computers can deliver teaching and learning material:

- CD-ROMs
- computer-assisted learning (CAL) packages
- the Internet via the World Wide Web.

Teaching and learning resources on CD-ROMs

CD-ROMs look like the CDs we buy for our hi-fi but, in addition to carrying music, they can also store digital video, images, sounds, text and programs. Many CD-ROMs are predominantly commercial and not suitable for higher education. CD-ROMs are available for a wide variety of topics from sophisticated courseware to telephone books and commercial or engineering databases with user-friendly interfaces.

Using Technology   1.3   Copyright and intellectual property rights

Beginner's Guide to Teaching and Learning Technology
http://www.icbl.hw.ac.uk/~william/cause/cause2.html

CD-ROMs can be used in a stand-alone mode or over a network, which allows many students to access the same material. You need to check with your supplier as you will need a site licence if you are thinking of making commercial CD-ROMs available in this way.

You can also put your own material on CD-ROM. Check whether your institution has this facility. Each CD-ROM can hold the equivalent of 250,000 pages (650Mb).

You could use a CD-ROM to store your lecture presentations, CAL packages, or databases (texts, images and sound). However, this is an archive medium and you will not be able to make changes to existing information (although you can append extra information). You can also take your slides to commercial photographic outlets to have your photos stored on Photo-CD. The quality of the slides in this medium is excellent when displayed on the computer. When viewed by a large group they can lose some of their definition, however, which may be a problem for medical slides where definition is vital.

Technology in Teaching	1.4	What kinds of material can you put on the computer?
Technology in Teaching	3	Using Internet resources
Technology in Teaching	5	Using the World Wide Web

CD-ROM titles include items such as interactive books for young children, resource collections (on Shakespeare, for example) encyclopedias, and other learning resources such as *The Way Things Work* by Dorling Kindersley. The market is currently dominated by CD-ROMs offering 'edutainment', but as the number of multimedia computers used in education rises, more educational titles are appearing. These resources allow the user to interrogate the information through various searching tools. The material is designed to be interrogated and in non-linear format, and enables rapid searches by keywords.

Teaching and learning resources with computer-assisted learning packages

Computer-assisted learning packages generally offer a fairly prescriptive route through a given set of material and offer a highly structured learning environment. They are effective as introductory teaching and learning material for a particular area.

These software packages can be bought through the UK higher education network from organizations such as ITTI (IT Teaching Initiative) and UCoSDA (Universities' and Colleges' Staff Development Agency, which disseminates ITTI materials). These have become outlets for much of the material produced under the Teaching and Learning Technology Programme (TLTP) which has funded various academics in the university sector to produce computer-assisted learning packages. The Computers in Teaching Initiative (CTI) is another source of knowledge for particular subject areas and the use of computers.

| Using Technology | 1.2.2 | What support is there for IT developments? |

Activity 3B Using CAL – educational considerations

Before using a CAL package, consider the following:

- Will the CAL package be comprehensive enough to enable your students to use it for independent study of a particular element in the course?

- If it is not comprehensive, how does this particular CAL package fit into your course as a whole?

- How will you run the course if this package is used?

- How will you support students?

- How will the students feel about using it?

Activity 3C   Departmental checklist: your constraints in using CAL

	Yes	No	Don't know
Hardware			
Does your department have sufficient computers available for CAL?			
Are these computers powerful enough? *			
Finances			
Is your department financially able to buy new computers?			
Is your department able to purchase courseware?			
Can your department pay for you to write material (eg by relieving you of contact hours or paying a research assistant for three months' work)?			
Networks and accessibility			
Is your department connected to the campus network or networked internally? You will need this to deliver material over the network.			
If you want to run your material on a local network in your department, can you provide a large enough training area?			
If you have to book public workstations instead, would you be deterred from using CAL?			
If you want to run your material on your departmental network, do you know how to set up your material or can someone do it for you?			
If you want to use the campus network, do you know the procedure?			
If you want to use the campus network, have you checked the rooms available for students accessing your material?			
If you use the campus network, have you checked availability of rooms for disabled student access?			
If you use the campus network, do your computing services people support your software? If not, what software do they support?			
Colleagues			
Do you know how your colleagues feel about CAL?			

   *Technology in Teaching   1.2   Choosing a computer

Computer-assisted learning packages today predominantly use text and graphics with some additional multimedia elements. They are generally produced in software packages known as authoring packages such as Asymmetrix's Toolbook, Owl's Guide and Apple's HyperCard. More expensive and commercial standard software includes Macromedia's AuthorWare and Director, and AimTech's IconAuthor.

These authoring systems are hypermedia (navigated by links across and within media) systems that allow 'hotspots' to be made in various places throughout the application linking the various components. You can navigate through the application using these hotspots as well as other navigational devices, as shown in Figure 3.5.

Figure 3.5   Hotspots linking documents (hypertext and hypermedia)

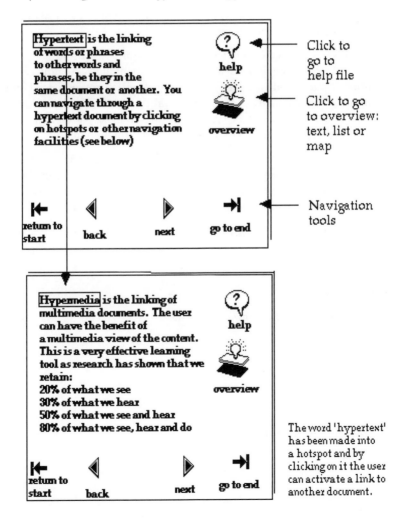

Computer-based learning packages produced in authoring software are sometimes referred to as courseware because they have specific application to certain courses. Authoring programs enable tutors and others to create learning packages specifically tailored to their own courses. Many have authoring languages associated with them, and you need to understand some very simple programming instructions to make the links on the hotspots. Here is an example of Toolbook Open Script code which will cause page 2 to be displayed when the hotspot is clicked on with the mouse.

```
On mouseUp
go page 2
End
```

The manuals supplied with authoring software will provide most of the information you need for such programming.

Most authoring software allows you to combine and link multimedia elements (text, sound, pictures, video) into a learning environment. It is generally easier to manipulate images outside the authoring package, so you will need other software to manipulate images, such as Microsoft's PaintBrush, Adobe PhotoShop or CorelDraw. Text, on the other hand, can be typed straight into these packages as with a word processor (except for MacroMedia AuthorWare Professional).

If you are thinking of producing your own CAL package, it is important to recognize that there is quite a steep learning curve. Not only are you learning how to use the authoring package, you are also capturing images and video as well as designing (plus piloting and evaluating) a whole new learning system.

If you are keen on producing your own CAL package, you will need to consider the following.

Authorware

http://www.macromedia.com/software/authorware/

Director

http://www.macromedia.com/software/director/

Macromedia Homepage

http://www.macromedia.com/software/

Asymetrix Homepage

http://www.asymetrix.com/

Toolbook User's Web

http://www.ets.bris.ac.uk/tosolini/tbkwww/tbkwww.html

IconAuthor

http://www.aimtech.com:80/iconauthor/

HyperCard Resource Page

http://www.glasscat.com/hypercard.cgi

CorelDraw 5.0 Trainer

http://www.keylearnsys.com/outlines/corel50.html

Adobe Photoshop (official site)

http://www.adobe.com/prodindex/photoshop/main.html

Figure 3.6 | *Choosing an authoring package*

Hardware
- What platform (PC or Mac) does it run on?
- What are the stated minimum hardware requirements? (Remember that it is always better to exceed these.)
- Can it be used over a network?

Technical
- How easy is it to incorporate images (video, scanned images)?
- How easy is it to incorporate sound?
- How much programming is needed to make simple links?

Support
- Is the package used nationally? Is there a user group for it?
- What training is available?
- Is the package supported and are there regular updates?
- Is anyone using the package in your institution?
- Where will it be used? If on campus network, will your computing services department support it? What about the licensing agreement?

Cost
- What is the cost of the package?
- What is the cost of the run-time version (ie the version that your users will need in order to run it)?
- Is there a CHEST (Consortium of Higher Education Software Team) agreement? (Through CHEST many authoring packages are made available to educational institutions at a lower price. See URL: *http://www.niss.ac.uk/chest/*)

ITTI (IT in Teaching Initiative) Web Pages
   http://www.icbl.hw.ac.uk/itti

Authorbase (a database of authoring systems on the World Wide Web)
   http://wwwetb.nlm.nih.gov/authorb/irx/index.html

Introduction to Multimedia on the World Wide Web
   http://info.mcc.ac.uk/CGU/SIMA/seminar/toc.html

Hofstetter (1995) *Multimedia literacy*[5]

The Emashe Group (1994) *Courseware in higher education evaluation 1: planning, developing and testing*[6]

McAteer and Shaw (1995) *The design of multimedia learning programs*[7]

Edwards, Howe and Smith (1994) *Advice on choosing an authoring package*[8]

Beginner's Guide to Teaching and Learning Technology
   http://www.icbl.hw.ac.uk/~william/cause/cause2.html

Teaching and learning resources on the World Wide Web

The Internet is an internationally networked group of services that allows us to:

– communicate with one another (email)
– view and download material on other computers around the world
– browse library catalogues, journal abstracts and citation indexes.

The World Wide Web (WWW) has made many of the more obscure services (Gopher, for example) more accessible, and has opened up the Internet to more users than ever before with its browsers that allow you to search on keywords across all WWW documents. The WWW provides an invaluable source of searchable information, and as it matures this information will become richer.

WWW documents are found by using their Internet address (known as a Uniform Resource Locator or URL). Documents are linked together to form a web of information which can be navigated by clicking on coloured hotspots. The WWW is a hypermedia system (ie clickable hotspots are links to other URLs containing multimedia documents). Text, however is the most prominent medium for WWW documents as other document types can take a long time to download. As networks become faster, this will change.

To gain access to the World Wide Web your computer will need an Internet address so you can make a connection. You will also need to download one of the browsers (viewers) so you will be able to view the documents. These browsers are freely available on the Internet. Finally, you will need either a Mac or a PC supporting a Windows environment. Ask your computing services staff to help you.

Figure 3.7   Some educational uses for the WWW, and the effort they require

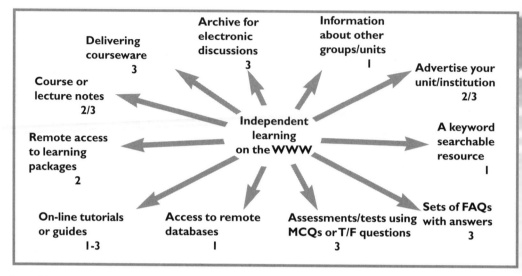

Key

FAQs   frequently-asked questions

MCQs   multiple-choice questions

T/F   true/false

Effort rating for using WWW
(assuming little or no experience in using WWW):

3   high

2   medium

1   low

Darby and Martin (eds) (1995) 'Using the Internet for teaching', *Active Learning* (2)[9]

Web Teaching Resources
http://www.lmu.ac.uk/lss/staffsup/webtr.htm
A collection of material to help you generate on-line learning material.

Accessing other peoples' resources
The WWW was originally designed to be used as a electronic publisher, and today there is a growing interest in using the WWW to disseminate journals electronically.

Case Study 1

The Political Science Discourse (PSD) is the bulletin of the Political Science Specialist Group of the ePSA-UK, launched in October 1995 with the support of the University of Southampton. Articles to be posted are screened to ensure that they are relevant to the bulletin and have sufficient literary qualities, but are not refereed. Comments are invited from peers once the article has been posted.

This bulletin can be seen at URL: *http://ilc.tsms.soton.ac.uk/webweek/politics.htm*

Case Study 2

Psycoloquy (ISSN 1055-0143) is a peer-reviewed interdisciplinary electronic journal sponsored by the American Psychological Association. It publishes articles and peer commentary in all areas of psychology as well as cognitive science, neuroscience, behavioural biology, artificial intelligence, robotics/vision, linguistics and philosophy. This is different from the PSD above, in that the articles are reviewed prior to posting.

The URL is:
http://cogsci.soton.ac.uk/~harnad/psyc.html

Case Study 3   An example of a home page

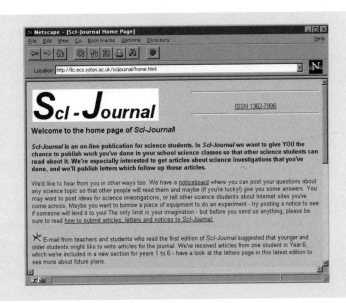

3.4 How computer technology can increase flexible access to learning resources

Essay and comments on electronic publishing
http://cogsci.soton.ac.uk/~harnad/THES/thes.html

Professor Harnad's papers on electronic publishing
http://cogsci.soton.ac.uk/~harnad/intpub.html

The Open Journal Project (funded by JISC's FIGIT initiative as a response to the Follett Report into Electronic Libraries)
http://journals.tsms.soton.ac.uk/

In addition to journals, most educational institutions are now advertising themselves on the WWW. They give information about their staff and their research activities, and sometimes you can find selected papers from these institutions. Most link to similar institutions or Web pages of interest to them. It is fairly easy therefore to form some kind of network of institutions in a particular area.

If you don't know the address (the URL) of a particular location you can search the WWW using keywords. On the Netscape browser, for example, there is a button called NetSearch which allows you to access a range of search tools. Or from File-Open in Netscape, type in the URL: *http://www.lycos.com*

Activity 3D   Check out some institutions

If you have access to the WWW, check out the following URLs:

The **CTI** has over 20 subject-based centres working to encourage the use of learning technologies in UK higher education. The CTI Support Service, based at the University of Oxford, co-ordinates the work of the centres, and acts as a focal point for activities relating to the use of computers in university teaching in the UK.
http://info.ox.ac.uk/cti/

TLTP (Teaching and Learning Technology Programme) information can be found on the Web. The site carries information about the Teaching and Learning Technology Programme and extracts from newsletters and information releases. It provides a central access point for information servers run by other projects within TLTP and related areas.
http://www.icbl.hw.ac.uk/tltp/

ILC (Interactive Learning Centre), University of Southampton, which is a central unit within the university primarily responsible for staff development in the area of IT for teaching and learning. They also offer external training workshops for the open hypermedia software, Microcosm.
http://ilc.tsms.soton.ac.uk/

The World Wide Web is increasingly being used as an authoring environment to produce learning materials and tutorial-type information.

Activity 3E **Accessing tutorial-type learning material**

Try some of the following:

The Complete Works of William Shakespeare
Allows you to search texts, look at frequently-asked questions and a glossary
>*http://the-tech.mit.edu:80/Shakespeare/works.html*

The Interactive Frog Dissection tutorial
Designed for use in high school biology classrooms, and initially developed by Richard Strauss, Jean Foss and Mable Kinzie
>*http://curry.edschool.Virginia.EDU:80/~insttech/frog/*

Kinship and Social Organization
An interactive tutorial from the University of Manitoba
>*http://www.umanitoba.ca/anthropology/kintitle.html*

NetSkills
A course of instruction on using the Internet produced with support from ITTI and Netskills
>*http://www.netskills.ac.uk/*

Disseminating your resources/course information via the Web
More and more institutions are using the WWW to disseminate information about themselves or to present course information or tutorial support.

If you want to write pages for the WWW you will need to learn how to mark up (tag) your documents. This is done with a programming language called HTML (hypertext mark-up language). It simply tags sections of the document to appear as heading, subheading and general page design. This allows your document to be read across any platform – PC, Mac or Unix.

Technology in Teaching   5   Using the World Wide Web

Case Study 4

Using the WWW to disseminate notes and course information

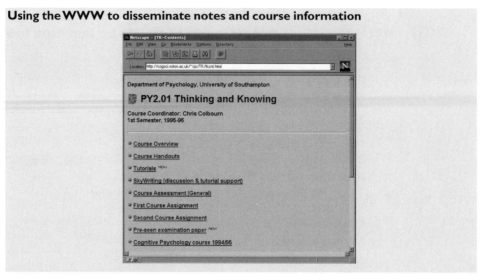

Words underscored are hotspots.

In addition to disseminating course information, Web pages can be authored to produce learning materials such as the example below:

Figure 3.8   *World Wide Web pages as a learning web*

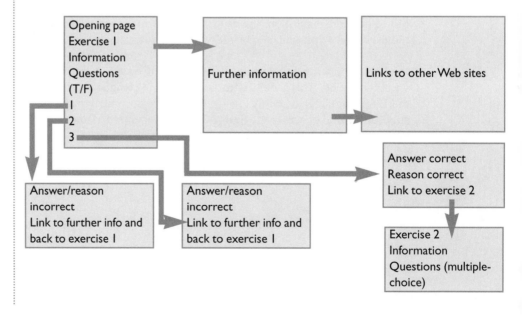

Multiple-choice questions and other question-and-answer types are also possible via the WWW.

Case Study 5

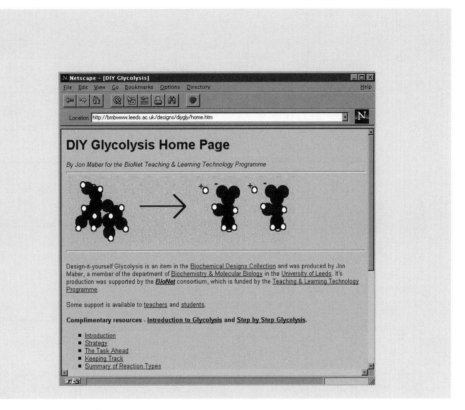

Using Technology	1.1.3	The impact of technology on the acquisition of knowledge
Technology in Teaching	5	Using the World Wide Web
Technology in Teaching	3.1	File transfer using ftp

Ford (1995) *Spinning the Web: how to provide information on the Internet*[10]

There is a plethora of Internet books in the shops and it is a matter of finding one that suits your level and needs.

3.5   Creating resource-based learning

Resource-based learning via the computer is a collection of multimedia teaching and learning materials ranging from simple text to computer-assisted learning programs (see Figure 3.9).

Figure 3.9   *A range of resource materials*

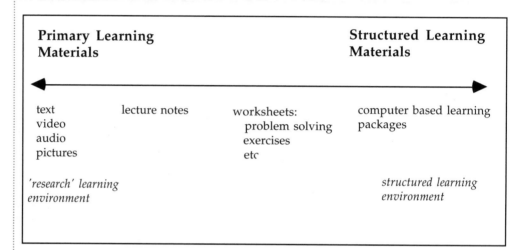

The learning resources presented in this continuum are not an exhaustive list of items, but simply serve to illustrate the diversity of material that can be considered.

Items under primary learning materials reflect a research learning style where students can interrogate a wide range of materials and construct their own knowledge: it resembles the notion of 'reading for a degree'. It is important to ensure, however, that students interrogate the resource purposefully, through tasks, to prevent aimless wandering through the material.

The other end of the continuum in Figure 3.9 represents a structured learning environment where there is a prescribed route through the material, very often with built-in exercises, simulations and questions. These structured environments are ideal for areas of knowledge that benefit from a more prescriptive instructional approach, such as procedures, rules and processes.

An important aim of higher education is that students will be able to manage their own learning through a research approach which is ultimately reflected in their becoming 'experts'. However, we cannot expect students to adopt this style of learning immediately, so structured learning materials are vital in the early stages. We can produce learning materials which are somewhere between primary and fully structured that help students towards a more research-based learning style: doing this will result in a rich and diverse resource base applicable to various stages and styles of learning.

Ideally, we need to be able to link together all these resources – be they primary resources or complete CAL programs – to form a rich hyperdocument. Some of the software concerned with the development of resource-based learning is Microcosm and STILE (Students' Teachers' Integrated Learning Environment).

3.5.1 *Microcosm as a hypermedia resource management tool*

Microcosm is the product of the University of Southampton Hypermedia Research Group, led by Professor Wendy Hall.

Essentially, Microcosm is a system for managing the documents in a resource collection. Any documents produced in a Windows environment (from simple text to computer-assisted learning programs) can be registered with Microcosm as a resource, and then linked to form a web of information. These documents – your resources – are not embedded in Microcosm: they are simply registered there (see Figure 3.10).

Figure 3.10 | *A simplified model of Microcosm as a digital resource centre*

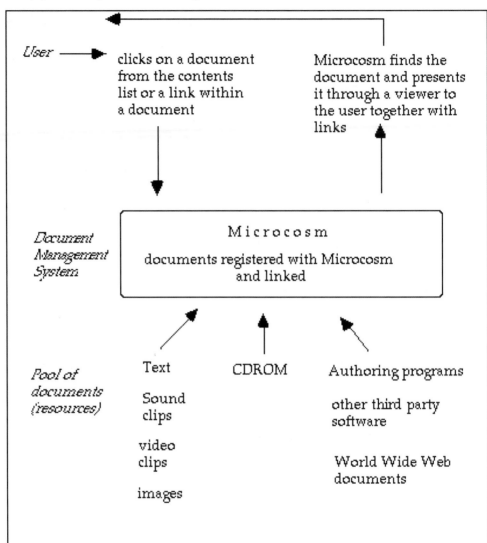

Once the documents are registered with Microcosm they can be structured to form a coherent body of knowledge. This is achieved by:
– a list of topic folders containing the resources (similar to a contents page in a book)
– by linking across the resources to form an integrated web of information.
– adding an instructional layer to the resources to guide students through the material via specific tasks, such as problem solving, case studies, simulations, exercises, etc.

Figure 3.11 | *Topic areas in a Microcosm application (document hierarchy)*

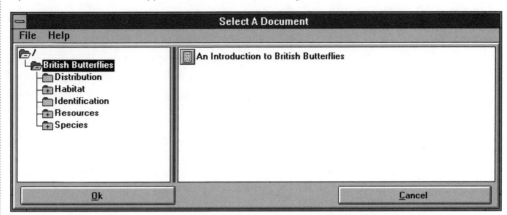

An important feature of Microcosm is that the information about the links is held separately from the documents themselves, in databases known as linkbases. So, while the documents are not embedded in Microcosm, neither is the link information embedded within the documents. These links offer the user a particular view of the resource and reflect your cognitive map of the information. A resource base can therefore have several linkbases reflecting different views of the same material, so you can link in various ways for distinct sets of learners. In addition, since documents are not embedded in Microcosm, they can still be used independently if you wish.

Document management software like Microcosm is an ideal mechanism for using existing CAL programs, grouping them together, and adding further material to suit your own course, with exercises, case studies etc to help and focus student learning. CAL programs (like products of TLTP and CTI initiatives) can now be integrated into courses rather than used only as independent stand-alone packages, which can lead to difficulty integrating them into the course as whole.

Using Technology   1.2.2   What support is there for IT development?

For more about Microcosm, see:
Microcosm Company: Multicosm
  http://www.multicosm.com/

For information about training courses for Microcosm, see:
Interactive Learning Centre, University of Southampton
  http://ilc.tsms.soton.ac.uk

3.5.2 STILE (Students' Teachers' Integrated Learning Environment)

STILE is a resource-based learning environment delivered via the World Wide Web (WWW) and the product of a TLTP project based at the University of Leicester and Loughborough. While Microcosm is essentially a document management system to organize and interrogate your resources, STILE is an easy-to-use resource retrieval system based on the ability to search a series of topics set up and owned by a tutor. Each topic is a WWW page with a title and descriptive paragraph. These topic areas link to other topics and to supporting resources. These are predominantly primary resources and essentially text or images. They can be produced by the tutor and made accessible via the WWW (given the necessary copyright clearance), or may be links to resources created by others and accessible via the WWW.

Figure 3.12 Linked topics in STILE

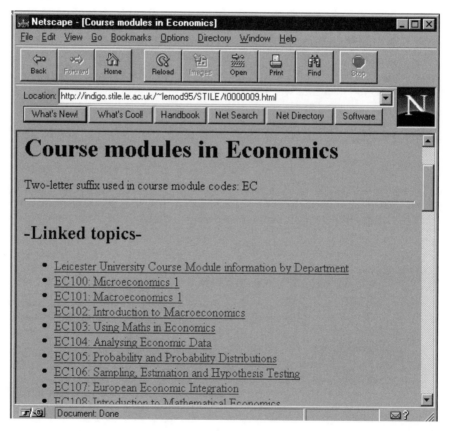

source: http://indigo.stile.le.ac.uk

The topics form an indexing function for the resources themselves, and are 'metadata' while the resources material itself is the 'data'.

STILE software tools comprise a topic editor and a converter . You can use the topic editor to create and edit topics without needing to know how to mark up a document for the WWW (ie without knowing the programming language HTML). The editors also allow topics to be linked to related topics and resources without knowledge of WWW terminology (such as URLs) as well as giving a uniform 'look and feel' which is essential for quick and easy student access.STILE pages have a 'search' facility for locating resources based on topics held on the STILE system. When you enter a name to search, the system will return information on the links you can follow and the order in which to access the data.

Figure 3.13   *STILE 'Buttons'*

source: http://indigo.stile.le.ac.uk

The STILE model has recently been extended to include a collaborative element where students interact via computer conferencing software or email. The Open University has also used STILE together with the computer conferencing system, FirstClass (developed by Softarc, and US Robotics 'Sportster' modems).

✗   Using Technology   4.4   Co-operative learning using computer conferencing

For more about STILE, see University of Leicester
http://indigo.stile.le.ac.uk/

 Underwood & Fitzpatrick (1995) *Focusing on resource-based learning: the STILE Project*[17]

3.6 *The movement towards the use of more learning technologies*

Various factors have led to an increased interest in the use of multimedia in education:

- increased numbers of students
- more diverse nature of student body
- teaching quality assessment procedures
- a reduction in the cost of technology
- increased 'user-friendliness' of computer software
- the growth in affordable authoring software
- the penetration of multimedia technology within society
- changing models of education from teacher-centred to student-centred strategies.

Our large and diverse body of students can be helped by information technology that gives them flexible access to key learning resources.

This flexibility will be crucial to future educational developments, especially in a culture that now expects learning to be a lifetime process rather than one normally confined to those aged under 21.

At present we need to carry out basic IT training to enable students to make the most of the software available. However, students in the future will have been brought up, at school or at home, using multimedia software packages either as games or as learning resources. Wherever they have encountered it, it will be an environment that is familiar to them. Industry is also taking advantage of the multimedia 'revolution' for use in desktop video conferencing, general marketing brochures distributed on CD-ROM, financial services, corporate training, electronic publishing, teleworking (people working from home using computers, modems and faxes), and many others.

Institutions of higher education, being part of society, are also influenced by these developments and our expectations, along with our students, will also change. We need to find out which parts of this technology fit our needs and then learn how to use them effectively to empower students and improve the quality of education.

There is a wide variety of learning technologies, and only a selected sample of them have been chosen for discussion. However, Figure 3.14 will give a quick overview of some of the key characteristics of a wider list.

Figure 3.14   Some characteristics of key learning technology

Medium	Production costs	Duplication costs	Audience type	Suitable content			Senses used
				cognitive	attitude	skill	
Printed materials	very low	very low	individual	excellent	fair	poor	sight
Audio-tape	low	low	group or individual	poor	good	poor	hearing
Slides	low	low	group or individual	fair	good	fair	sight
Video	medium	low	group or individual	fair	good	good	sight + hearing
CAL	medium	low	individual	excellent	poor	good	sight
Interactive multimedia	very high	medium	group or individual	excellent	good	good	sight + hearing
Virtual reality	very high	medium	individual	good	excellent	excellent	sight + hearing, body, movement
Simulation	high	high	group or individual	good	good	excellent	sight + hearing, body, movement
WWW	low	low	individual	good	fair	poor	sight, possibly hearing
Email	low	low	group or individual	good	good	poor	sight
Computer conferencing	medium	low	group or individual	good	good	poor	sight

Adapted from: SCET (1994) Technologies in learning[18]

> Choosing which technology to use will depend on its availability in your institution, together with your interest in pursuing it.

Activity 3F   Issues to consider when using digital teaching and learning resources

1   *Will you need photographs or slides?*   **Yes** ☐   **No** ☐

If 'yes', how will you process these and how will students gain access to them?

Will you use a Photo-CD or scanned images?

Do you have a budget for this?

What is the educational value of using pictures?

2   *Will you need sound?*   **Yes** ☐   **No** ☐

If 'yes', will you use audio cassettes or digitized sound?

Do you know how to get sound digitized? If not, can you find out easily?

Do you need high-quality sound that you can only get from a studio recording, or will a lesser quality (by recording directly into your PC or Mac from a microphone) be sufficient?

If you are using digital sound, how will you integrate it with other resources?

What is the educational value of using sound?

3   *Will you need animation or video?*   **Yes** ☐   **No** ☐

If 'yes', do you already have the animation or do you need someone to produce it?

Can you digitize video, or will you need help? If 'yes', where from?

Can your video be easily chopped into one- or two-minute clips to illustrate particular points?

What is the educational value of your video?

4   *How about interactivity with your resources?*

How would you like your students to interact with your material?

- drill and practice

- predictive exercises

- questions (T/F, or multiple-choice, or open ended)

- problem solving

- case studies

- simulation

What do you expect your students to gain from your materials? How does the interactivity fulfil this?

5   *Do your students require support?*

   Yes ☐   **No** ☐

The answer should be 'yes'. Build in a support programme for your
students: clearly state course objectives, assignments and what is expected
of the student. Give students an overview of the department's hierarchy so
they know who to call when necessary.

6   *Do you want to produce a CAL program yourself?*

   Yes ☐   **No** ☐

If 'yes', be prepared for a lot of work. The Open University has found it better to establish
course teams. The course also has a wider anchor in the department with this model. If
'no', contact TLTP, CTI or UCoSDA for packages (see Teaching and Learning 1.2.2).

7   *Do you want to assemble a digital resource centre?*

   Yes ☐   **No** ☐

If 'yes', you need to decide on the software you will need to use to manage your resources.

You need to locate suitable CAL programmes to include in your resource. You don't need
to produce everything yourself.

You will need to get all your other resources digitized, with video and sound clips where
suitable. Do you know where to get this done?

Decide on your educational strategy: exercises, tests, cases, problem
solving, etc that will draw on your resources.

Many universities and colleges have set up centres, units or departments to help staff
use new technology. The University of Berkeley, in the US, has a central unit: the
Instructional Techology Program. This unit offers, for example, staff training in the
use of learning technologies, methods of getting staff involved and instructional
resources on the web. Northwestern University offers workshops on technology in
teaching and learning to their own staff and those external to the university. In
Australia, Queensland University of Technology offers a comprehensive website on
how technology can be used in education, what technology is available, how
technology can be integrated into the curriculum, what help is available and how it is
related to learning. In the UK similar units can be found within universities.

For those interested in developing an institutional policy on the use of technology in
learning, it may be worth taking a look at the University of Berkeley's Instructional
Technology Subcommittee documents that have been publicized on the World Wide
Web.

Instructional Technology Program (University of Berkeley)

http://www.itp.berkeley.edu/

Technology in Teaching and Learning at Northwestern University

http://www.new.edu/at/training/tilt/

California State University, CHICO

http://www.csuchico.edu/tlp/

Queensland University of Technology

http://www.tals.dis.qut.au/tlow/tlow.htm

New Chalk

A Bi-Weekly featuring Instructors' use of networked technologies

http://www.unc.edu/courses/newchalk/archive/ncarchive.html

Instructional Technology Subcommitee at the University of Berkeley

http://socrates.berkeley.edu/~cccpb-it/

University of Bristol: Institute for Learning and Research Technology (ILRT)

They initiate multimedia based learning projects. They also have a learning technology support servicew for in-house teaching staff. Check out the ILRT 'projects' link.

http://www.ilrt.bris.ac.uk/

University of Leicester

Check out the 'Learning Technology Group' link.

http://www.le.ac.uk/

Using Technology 2.4 Assessing large groups

Remember that you can use each of the digital resources in isolation, in a computer-assisted learning package, or linked together as a resource base. In all modes the material can be made available across the network for flexible student access.

If you don't want to do any of that, either search the World Wide Web and see what you can find, or buy commercially produced CD-ROMs.

Beginner's Guide to Teaching and Learning Technology
http://www.icbl.hw.ac.uk/~william/cause/cause2.html

References for Chapter 3

[1] Source: Gibbs (1989), 'Designing learning packages: Module 8' in *Certificate in Teaching in Higher Education by Open Learning*, Oxford Centre for Staff Development

[2] Race, Phil (1992), *53 Interesting ways to write open learning materials*, Technical and Educational Services Ltd, 37 Ravenswood Road, Bristol BS6 6BW, England

[3] Rowntree, Derek (1994), *Preparing materials for open, distance and flexible learning: an action guide for teachers and trainers*, Kogan Page, London

[4] Warren, Lorraine (1993), *Understanding IT: computer-based presentations*, CVCP/USDU, Sheffield

Although she does not refer to how we can use multimedia components, Lorraine Warren gives a good account of what computer-based presentations are and some help with the use of colour. There is also a demonstration disk.

For a copy contact UCoSDA tel: 0114 272 5248 or email: ucosda@sheffield.ac.uk

[5] Hofstetter, Fred (1995), *Multimedia literacy*, McGraw-Hill, London

A good introductory book for multimedia. It comes with a CD-ROM (by Patricia Fox) which allows you to carry out the interactive exercises on authoring as set out in the book. There is also an instructor's guide to accompany the book.

[6] The Emashe Group (1994), *Courseware in higher education evaluation 1: planning, developing and testing*, UCoSDA, Sheffield

In addition to evaluation, this booklet has a detailed checklist of authoring software characteristics. To order, contact UCoSDA tel: 0114 272 5248, email: ucosda@sheffield.ac.uk

[7] McAteer, Erica and Robin Shaw (1995), *The design of multimedia learning programs*, University of Glasgow, available from UCoSDA, Sheffield

[8] Edwards, John, Gilbert Howe and Fred Smith (1994), *Advice on choosing an authoring package*, Educational Technology Service, University of Bristol (available from UCoSDA, ucosda@sheffield.ac.uk)

[9] Darby, Jonathan and Joyce Martin (eds), 'Using the Internet for teaching', *Active learning* (2), July 1995

[10] Ford, Andrew (1995), *Spinning the Web: how to provide information on the Internet*, International Thompson

[11] Nielsen, Jakob (1995), *Multimedia and hypertext: the Internet and beyond*, Academic Press Inc., London (section on Microcosm under Open Hypertext, p. 146)

[12] Einon, Geoff, 'Build "open" multimedia apps with Microcosm 3.0, *PC Magazine*, May 1995

[13] Hall, Wendy (1994), 'Ending the tyranny of the button' IEEE *Multimedia* (1), pp. 60–68

[14] Jonassen, David, 'Hypertext's Cognitive Tools' in Kommers, Piet, D. Jonassen and T. Mayes, (eds) (1990), *Cognitive tools for learning*, NATO-ASI Series, Springer Verlag, Berlin, pp. 147–148

[15] Duffy, Thomas and David Jonassen (eds) (1992), *Constructivism and the technology of instruction: a conversation*, Lawrence Erlbaum Associates, London

[16] Knowledge Tree: Available from UCoSDA tel: 0114 272 5248, email: ucosda@sheffield.ac.uk
It is also available by ftp from *http://ibis.nott.ac.uk/software/kt-available.html*

[17] Underwood, Jean and Simon FitzPatrick, 'Focusing on resource-based learning: the STILE Project', Journal of Educational Library Studies, March 1995

[18] SCET (1994), *Technologies in learning*, SCET Publishing Ltd.

4 Using computers to communicate with and between students

Once the technology is embedded in a campus, and the communication links provided, it is a relatively simple but conceptually significant step to link geographically distant learning communities into a single 'virtual learning community'. Similarly, the developing technological and communications infrastructure enables individuals to enter… 'virtual communities', to exchange ideas and work collaboratively on projects.

Greville Rumble's foreword in Robin Mason (ed) (1993), *Computer conferencing: the last word…*,
Beach Holm Publishers Ltd, Victoria, British Columbia

4.1 *Some technologies for communicating with each other*

British universities are linked by a computer network called JANET (Joint Academic Network). This allows lecturers, via an electronic mail (email) address, to write messages to colleagues and students within and outside a particular university. Fellow academics can communicate with each other all over the world.

Some other nations have networks like JANET, but most rely on commercial networks to connect their academic institutions to the Internet, and negotiate their own arrangements with network companies.

In addition to email, there are discussion groups known as mailbases. Mailbases are set up and 'owned' by an administrator who is able to delete any offensive messages or deal with anyone breaking 'netiquette' (behaviour code for the Internet). Mailbases can also be archived so participants can trace information and people. This is now being achieved using the World Wide Web.

Computer conferencing is another type of communications package that is very similar to email. However, it is far more sophisticated and allows for electronic 'areas' to be set aside for particular discussions. It can also track conversation threads, enabling you to keep track of discussions.

This section examines some of the uses of email, mailbases and computer conferencing as a way of keeping in contact with students. Information can be 'posted' via the system to encourage them to work co-operatively even if they cannot be together physically. These are all asynchronous (participation which is independent of time or place) modes of communication that increase the flexibility of students to interact with other groups with whom they may not be in face-to-face contact. As educators, we need to learn how to manage these electronic groups and re-assess our teaching strategy accordingly.

Figure 4.1 Computers in education: communications

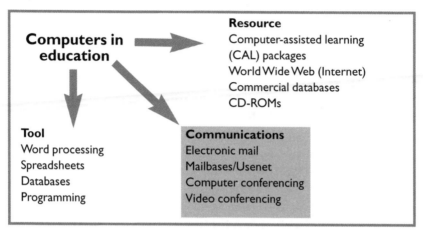

4.2 Communicating via email

Email is a relatively low-effort technology: once you have a computer that can receive email on your desk and you've learned to use it, the major effort is over.

Activity 4A Do you use email?

	Yes	No	Would like to
I use electronic mail (email) regularly	☐	☐	☐

Feedback

If you answered 'Yes', go to table 4B

If you answered 'No' or 'Would like to', go to table 4C

Activity 4B How do you use email?

	Yes	No	Would like to
1 I use email to talk to colleagues in the university	☐	☐	☐
2 I use email to communicate with my students	☐	☐	☐

3 I sometimes use email instead of holding meetings

☐ ☐ ☐

4 I encourage students to communicate with each other via email

☐ ☐ ☐

5 I have joined at least one mailbase

☐ ☐ ☐

Feedback

If you answered 'No' to any of the above, can you think of how extended use of email could help you: email instead of memos, email agenda and minutes for meetings, sending course information to students, etc?

If you answered 'Yes', you are well on your way to being an email junkie. Make sure you see your colleagues and students from time to time!

Activity 4C   **Why don't you use email?**

	Yes	No
1 We need to connect to more network points	☐	☐
2 I need to have a computer on my desk, or one that can receive email	☐	☐
3 The system is too slow and cumbersome	☐	☐
4 I used to use it, but it broke down and I haven't been able to get it fixed	☐	☐
5 I used to use it, but got too much mail, so I stopped using it	☐	☐
6 I haven't got round to learning how to use it	☐	☐
7 I just don't want to use it	☐	☐

Feedback

If you answered 'Yes' to questions 1–4, then you are hindered from using email for technical reasons. It may be worth finding out how others feel about this and, as a group, ask for a better service and more computers. Make out a case for integrating email into your teaching and administrative duties.

If you answered 'Yes' to question 5, you may have had a bad experience on mailbases which can flood your mailbox if you aren't careful. Dealing with large quantities of mail can be daunting; just be ruthless and delete. If it's important, they will mail you back. When you go on holiday, email your list asking them not to mail you, and suspend your membership from mailbases.

If you have answered 'Yes' to questions 6 and 7, you are probably sceptical of its value to you. Why don't you talk to others who use it regularly or sign up on the next email course at your institution?

! If you are going to use electronic communication in any way in your teaching, you should have on your desk a computer that can receive email. This computer should be either a PC with Windows or a Mac: both these will allow you to 'click' between your current work and email messages without having to close down your work.

Email can be used to write personal messages to colleagues and public messages for a specified group of people (ie a broadcast message). Email has a mechanism for making broadcasting easier. You don't have to write the whole list of people you want to send the message to every time: you can set up an 'alias' which is a group name for that list. For example, if you want to email everyone on course CO123, you can write out the list of email addresses, give it an alias name – like CO123 – and when you send each email you simply use that alias name for your message to be broadcast to the whole group. The ability to create public messages so easily makes email an ideal medium for group communication.

Figure 4.2   Broadcast and private messaging using email

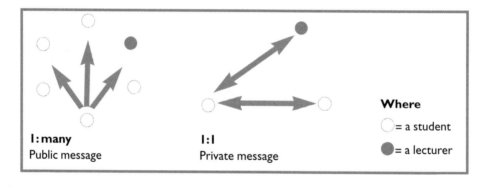

1:many
Public message

1:1
Private message

Where
◯ = a student
● = a lecturer

Technology in Teaching   4.1   Electronic mail

4.2.1 Using email in your teaching

Before you start in a serious way to integrate email into your teaching, you need to establish your starting point.

Activity 4D   **What's your starting point?**

		Yes	No
1	Is the campus-wide network wide enough?	☐	☐
2	Is the system reliable?	☐	☐
3	Are faults dealt with quickly?	☐	☐
4	Are your students entitled to have an email address?	☐	☐
5	Are there enough computers for students to access?	☐	☐
6	Do you have on your desk a computer that can receive email?	☐	☐
7	Do your teaching assistants have easy access to a computer that receives email?	☐	☐
8	Can your students already use email?	☐	☐
9	Can your teaching assistants use email?	☐	☐

Feedback

If you answered 'Yes' to all of the questions above, you are in a good position to exploit email as much as possible.
If you answered 'No' to questions 1–4, these are service issues and you would need to press for improved services centrally.

If you answered 'No' to questions 5–7, there will be a problem accessing email. Find out the ratio of computers to students in public areas. You may have to work out a case for increasing this ratio. Discuss this at departmental meetings. Do you have an IT strategy in your institution? If so, it may be worth reading. Do you have contacts on relevant committees?

If you answered 'No' to questions 8 and 9, you may need to train your students and teaching assistants. This does not necessarily mean that it has to be you who does the training. Ask your local computing services if they offer email courses for staff and students. If so, book your people onto such a course as soon as possible.

If all your students are on email it gives you the opportunity to contact them individually and as a group exactly when you want to. Contact this way can be spontaneous and timely.

It is important, if you are using this method of communication regularly, to insist that your students check their email daily or at least twice a week.

Encouraging student–student emailing
By distributing student email lists you can encourage self-help groups to form that may have difficulty meeting otherwise. Your students will then need to know how to make alias groups so they can communicate with their help group or the class as a whole.

Using email effectively in groups is a transferable skill, and one that your students are going to need, so encourage them to use it now.

Technology in Teaching	4.1	Electronic mail
Technology in Teaching	2.4	How do you get connected?

Electronic discussions
Email is not the ideal mechanism for an electronic seminar, hypermail (see 4.3.2) or a computer conferencing system (see 4.4) is far superior. However, if you don't have access to a computer conferencing system and you want to encourage discussion groups, why not try email?

Before using email, ask yourself:
- How will this benefit the students and improve the existing course?
- How will the technology affect my role?
- How will the technology affect the students?

You will also need to ensure that your students:
- are entitled to an email address
- know how to get one
- have access to computers with email facilities
- are trained to use email
- are given all the email addresses of the group.

If you are going to incorporate the use of email into your course, make sure your students know what you expect and how the group is likely to function.

- Will a topic be discussed? Is contribution to the discussion mandatory and, if so, do students know this? How often do you expect students to contribute? Is there a time limit? Do you expect any outcome as a result of these discussions? How will you encourage the reticent ones to take an active part? Will contributions be assessed?

- Will it be used as a 'clinic' where difficult topics are discussed? Will you encourage students to ask and answer the questions as in a self-help group? When will you intervene? Do students know you want to 'listen' in? Will you then be able to feed this information back into the course, and will students know this?

In an electronic medium the role of the tutor is referred to as the 'moderator'. In this role you check the discussions, put people back on the right track, suggest a particular line of thought and encourage those who are quiet – possibly with a personal email to coax them on. The degree of control you have can vary, however. You can have a high central prominence where you control the discussions, or you can observe from a distance, commenting only when needed.

Using Technology   4.5   Managing electronic 'virtual' groups

Using email to keep in touch with teaching assistants (TAs)

Once you have decided to use email, you are likely to need to include your teaching assistants: as groups get larger you need to arrange for TAs to deal with some of them. This becomes more of a management issue than a teaching issue. Getting everyone together to have meetings can be problematic, so why not use email?

You could set up a group name for your TAs on a particular course and mail them via a 'public' (1: many) message. Last-minute details can be communicated quickly in this way as well as the group serving as a forum for discussion. Encourage your TAs to set up an alias group name so that they can also send one message to the whole group, whether that is the 'TA group' or their 'student group'.

Handling your email

You may be reticent to open up full email contact with your students for fear of being flooded with mail. If this is indeed the case you may have to be straight with your students and say that you cannot answer all their email. You could also develop a 'filing' system for student email. In the subject area of the email message you could ask them to start with the code of the course. This way you could search/find/file according to course codes and read messages later. This may allow you to answer many questions en bloc, in a public (1: many) manner as a 'frequently-asked-questions' (FAQ) message.

If you do not want students to have open and direct access to you, you could set up a hierarchy or a buffer between you and your students, using teaching assistants (see Figure 4.3).

Figure 4.3   An email hierarchy for communicating with students and TAs

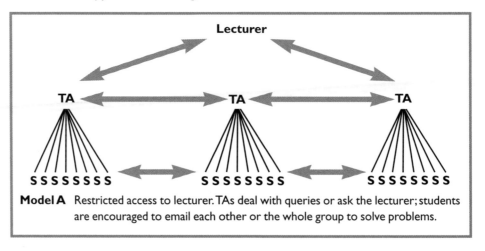

Model A Restricted access to lecturer. TAs deal with queries or ask the lecturer; students are encouraged to email each other or the whole group to solve problems.

Figure 4.4   Open-access model between lecturer, TAs and students

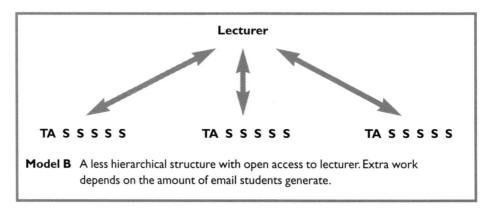

Model B A less hierarchical structure with open access to lecturer. Extra work depends on the amount of email students generate.

4.3   *Participating in electronic discussion groups*

4.3.1   *Mailbases*

Mailbases are national and international groups that use the email system to send messages to everyone who has registered with them. Joining a group allows you to discuss topics of common interest with many people around the world. A message sent to the mailbase address goes to everyone registered with that group. If the group is large and active, you could end up with a lot of email!

Alternatively, you can simply be an observer with this group, contribute to the discussion or ask for information. There is no one cajoling you along: the success or failure of the mailbase depends entirely on its members. Mailbases can become a resource of current ideas and solutions to particular problems. You can keep track of topical issues very easily.

When you join a mailbase, keep all the information you receive from the administrator about leaving the group. You may find in a short while that you are inundated with email of no interest to you, in which case knowing how to 'unsubscribe' quickly will be vital!

If there is a mailbase that you think will interest your students, email them some information about it plus instructions for joining. Warn them that they may find they have a lot of email to deal with and that they should be prepared for that.

Many busy mailbases are now putting their emails on to a World Wide Web site. The mailbase you join will give you instructions about this. The mailbase WWWEDU (World Wide Web in education), for example, has the WWW address, with an archive of email messages:
> *http://www.fwl.org/hyper-discussions/wwwedu-l/*

For computer-mediated collaborative learning, see the WWW address:
> *http://www.mailbase.ac.uk/lists-a-e/cm-collab-learning/*

To find out what mailbases exist, the WWW address to try is:
> *http://www.mailbase.ac.uk/*
> *or email: mailbase-admin@uk.ac.mailbase*

Technology in Teaching   4.2   Mailing lists

4.3.2 *Hypermail*

Electronic mail makes it possible for people to discuss a number of topics simultaneously over a period of days, or weeks. However, this can get confusing, especially when a number of different 'conversations' are going on at the same time.

With computer conferencing software, it is possible to organize the contributions of participants by:
- subject (so that you can easily follow a discussion on a particular topic: a 'thread')
- author (to make it easy to see what particular people are saying)
- date (the normal way messages would be recorded).

Hypermail is software which is used to structure email discussions in this way (subject/author/date). Email messages sent to a special email address are periodically converted into a mail archive which is in HTML format and can be browsed by all interested parties (subject to access controls) as a World Wide Web document. The Hypermail software runs on a variety of Unix platforms and is available free of charge for non-commercial use.

For further details see URL:
> *http://www.eit.com/software/hypermail/hypermail.html*

Here is an example of a Hypermail WWW page:

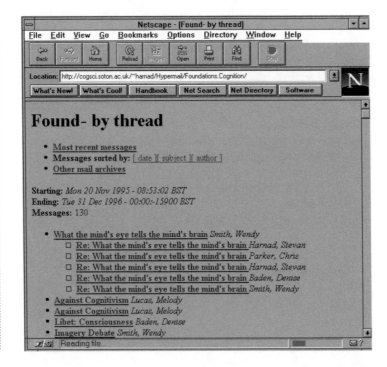

Where the text is bold, there are 'hotspots' allowing you to open the mail or sort it according to thread, subject and author.

 Technology in Teaching　　4.4　　Computer conferencing

4.4　*Co-operative learning using computer conferencing*

Computer conferencing is an ideal tool for collaborative or co-operative learning. It's an electronic environment with various 'areas' set aside for small group work, large group work, socializing and resources. As with email, computer conferencing is an asynchronous mode of communication with communication taking place at the convenience of the participant.

Co-operative learning can be viewed on several dimensions (McConnell, D 1994): structure, teacher control, moderation of learning, learner motivation, learning content and assessment. How much control do you, as a teacher, have over the course? Are your students essentially motivated internally or are they motivated externally by you and the exam system? Is the course content seen as objective information that students need to digest or do they have some say? Where you are along these dimensions depends on the kind of teacher you are, the circumstances under which you are teaching, your students and to some extent the academic discipline.

 Activity 4E　**Dimensions of co-operative learning**

Tick along the scale where you are now with regard to your teaching. Try this activity with a first-year course and then with a third-year course.

highly structured course	**Structure**	no course structure
high	**Teacher control**	low
external	**Moderation of learning**	internal
external	**Learner motivation**	internal
curriculum-based	**Learning content**	learner-based
unilateral by teacher	**Assessment**	unilateral by student

Source: McConnell (1994), p. 21

Feedback

If your marks are predominantly towards the right side for your first-year group, have you prepared them for this kind of education? They need to learn how to be managers of their own education as this does not come automatically. Think about the support you may need to give this group.

Your position should have moved more towards the right-hand end of the continuum (unless you were there already!) as you considered a third-year group of students. Did you plunge your third-year students into this mode of learning, or have you prepared them for it over the first two years? If your marking remained towards the left, is this due to internal or external reasons? This may be worth examining.

Your position on these scales will determine how much control you feel you need over your students and how you design an on-line course (or any course) using computer conferencing.

McConnell, David (1994) *Implementing computer-supported co-operative learning*[1]

Co-operative learning allows your students to take some control of their learning, working together producing joint products rather than in competition, regurgitating facts presented by the lecturer or books. It is process oriented rather than product oriented and very different from traditional approaches to teaching in higher education.

Computer conferencing systems

Computer conferencing software, course information and messages are located on a central computer known as a server. You and your students will need computers with appropriate software that can connect to this server. When you log on to the system you are automatically connected to this server and can access information you have the right to see. If you wish, you can copy this information to your own computer; this is called 'downloading'. You can also leave messages there for others to see when they log on. Putting messages and information on to the server is known as 'uploading'.

When you log on you are told how many messages you have received since you last logged on. Depending on the software, you will probably also be able to search previous entries on author, title or other mechanisms. Threads of discussions are also maintained so you can track back through a particular topic of discussion.

Computer conferencing systems are text-based interactive systems. 'Areas' or 'conferences' are set up by the moderator/tutor. A course can have several conference areas, some being accessible to the whole group and others that are specific to a small group (or set). A typical example would be:

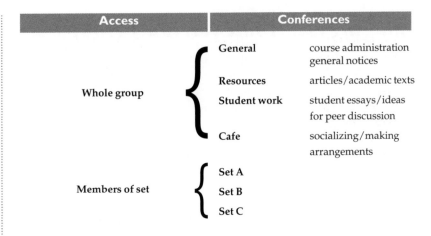

Access		Conferences	
Whole group	**General**	course administration general notices	
	Resources	articles/academic texts	
	Student work	student essays/ideas for peer discussion	
	Cafe	socializing/making arrangements	
Members of set	**Set A**		
	Set B		
	Set C		

Some examples of computer conferencing systems are:

- FirstClass
  http://www.nashville.net/~qic95/WCC/fcweb/firstclass.html
- Lotus Notes
  http://www.lotus.com/home/notes.htm

 Technology in Teaching   4.4   Computer conferencing

Knowledge Tree, produced by the Bioinformatics Group at the University of Nottingham, England, is a collaborative tool for student discussion. Discussions can be stored in a knowledge base (knowledge garden) to be accessed later. There is also a concept thesaurus that allows conversations to follow threads. This enables a collaborative tool to be embedded within a hypertext resource. The universities of Nottingham and Southampton are exploring ways of incorporating it into Microcosm open hypermedia system as a live debate medium that can utilize the hypertext linking mechanism. This technology shows the merging of communications and resources.

 Using Technology   3.5.2   Adding communications to resource-based learning

 Knowledge Tree
http://ibis.nott.ac.uk/software/kt.html

Computer-Mediated Communication Magazine
http://www.rpi.edu/~decemj/cmc/mag/

4.5 Managing electronic (virtual) groups

When we interact on-line – whether by computer conference, email or mailbase – we are interacting in a virtual group; the group doesn't physically exist in one time and one place but is disparate and interacting asynchronously. Although we are still the same people, we are interacting in a new way, and this new way has to be managed differently.[4]

First let us look at the essential differences between face-to-face and electronic groups.

Figure 4.5   Communication in face-to-face and electronic groups

Face-to-face group	Electronic group
Channels of communication Uses a variety of channels: words, intonation, posture, etc to convey meaning and emotion.	**Channels of communication** A single channel: textual. This is why some see electronic groups as cold and impersonal. Emotion can be conveyed by symbols or 'smileys' (see below).
Mode of communication Synchronous: all are physically gathered in a given place at a given time.	**Mode of communication** Asynchronous: time and place for communication is at the discretion of individuals.
Essentially verbal, but with a great deal of non-verbal cues like intonation, posture, facial expressions and hand movements.	The mode of communication is a mixture between verbal and written text. This is now known as 'interactive writing'. Email texts can be spontaneous, and can tolerate misspellings and grammatical errors as with spoken texts. Email can also support thought-out prose as in written texts.
Social cues to communication Members of a face-to-face group are aware of social cues to status in their environment and with their group leader.	**Social cues to communication** Electronic groups experience a social levelling, as many of the cues to social status are removed.
Turn taking You need to wait your turn in a face-to-face group and you may even miss the opportunity to say something.	**Turn taking** There is no need to wait your turn in electronic groups; you contribute when you feel like with either a spontaneous or a thought-out response.

| Technology in Teaching | 4.1 | Electronic mail |
| Technology in Teaching | 2.4 | How do you get connected? |

We are having to 'manage' groups in an electronic environment, operating with significantly fewer communication cues than in a face-to-face set-up. We only have typewritten textual material and some mood symbols such as the following (you may need to look at the page sideways to see them):
- :) happy
- :(sad/frown
- ;) wink

Some issues relating to interacting in electronic groups
Electronic communications differ from spoken and other written forms, and a specific style is evolving. Before you start, you may need to consider the following points:
- What you say may be a permanent record.
- Think about getting the register right. There can be some confusion as to whether this is a formal textual medium or a 'letter to my friend'. In fact, it's both and what happens depends on the group.
- Criticism can be all too easily 'dished out' because you are not face to face.
- Electronic communication can be blunter than face-to-face communications since face-saving devices – like not embarrassing someone – may not operate so strongly.
- 'Is there anybody out there?': some users feel very isolated using this medium, especially if a question is not answered.

All these factors, and more, need to be dealt with early on in electronic group communications. You need to find ways to support reticent participants and positively acknowledge their contributions.

Some ground rules could be developed for all participants:
- Acknowledge critical messages from participants even if you can't give a full answer at that time. Critical messages may include asking for information or putting up an idea for discussion.
- Be critical by all means, but don't overdo it in a public medium.
- Pick out good points as well as bad points.
- Thank people for responding to your request or helping you out and say what you thought was useful in their comments; this gives valuable feedback.
- Keep to the topic of the conference and don't fill up conferences with irrelevant messages.

These ground rules will help you to set up a successful collaborative learning environment. You need to decide how much control you need to exercise, and how far you can step back: this will depend on your students and your course.

Activity 4F   Five questions about managing electronic groups

1 **Are your support mechanisms in place for students?** Yes → Fine

    No → Think about:

    – induction sessions
    – face-to-face days for distance students
    – well-prepared study guides.

2 **Is the function of the group explicit to you and your students?** Yes → How does the electronic group relate to the course as a whole?

    No → Is this:

    – a discussion group?
    – a problem-solving group?
    – a decision-making group?
    – a role-play group?
    – a peer-evaluation group?
    – a self-help group?

    If it is a mixture, will there be a time limit for each phase?

3 **Does your group know what to expect?** Yes → Fine

    No → Then:

    – give them a clear explanation of procedures for decision-making and/or problem solving
    – make it clear how often you expect them to log on.

    Will their contributions be assessed? How?

    – are there sanctions for people who don't contribute?
    – think about setting a time limit on specific group (set) discussions.

4 **Are you clear about your role in this electronic group?** Yes → Fine

    No → Decide on the function of the group and your role in it.

5 Does your group have a function apart from keeping in contact?

No
For a social group there is little you need to do. Asking how everyone is getting on and for course feedback could be useful.

Yes
You will need to moderate it to maintain its focus. Decide on your role:

- to maintain group momentum, encourage, give confidence – a private email to find out why someone is not contributing will make them feel noticed

- as a mentor: helping with ideas, introducing new ideas and avoiding misconceptions

- as a director: leading the discussion, setting the limits, correcting misconceptions and asking for opinions.

In this mode you will be the centre of discussions and will need to put in a lot of time to keep it going as it will stagnate when you stop contributing.

- as an observer: you must let your students know if you do this. If you need to intervene, decide on a strategy.

Case Study 1 **Cranfield School of Management**

In 1988 the Cranfield School of Management used networking on its two-year MBA course. The networking grew from the decision to introduce spreadsheets and word processing into their course. Since the course is essentially case-based and students need to work together on cases (which they did previously by phone and fax), computer conferencing offered a more flexible alternative. Cranfield purchased laptop computers which it loaned out to students together with a modem, printer and software. A special group deal was negotiated with Dialcom (the Internet provider) for restricted access to Telecom Gold for all the students. The management school pays all the Dialcom costs – students pay only for the telephone call to the nearest PSS node. The student fees for such a course are adjusted accordingly.

4.6 Considerations for open and distance learning courses

Open and distance education is no longer restricted to the Open University, the Open College or company training schemes. It is becoming an ever-increasing part of traditional universities and other higher educational establishments. It is sometimes referred to as tele-university or telematics.

Stand-alone open learning provides material for students to work on without a tutor being present, in their own time, alone or collaboratively with fellow students. This can take place on or off campus. Such learning 'on campus' can be loosely referred to as open learning while 'off campus' and at greater distances it is called distance learning. This is a form of education traditionally associated with the Open University.

As student numbers increase, university buildings become more disparate and with a growing need to maximise income, more universities are offering distance courses to students who cannot travel to the courses they want, or more flexibly arranged courses, through an open learning scheme that allows those who have domestic or professional restrictions to study. These methods of course delivery, coupled with new advances in learning technology, are becoming serious alternatives to traditional university courses. New technology is adding a varied dimension to independent learning materials with multimedia computer-based learning packages, and Internet facilities for email, computer and video conferencing and World Wide Web as a distance learning environment with resources and archived communication (hypermail).

Beginner's Guide to Teaching and Learning Technology[2]
http://www.icbl.hw.ac.uk/~william/cause/cause2.html

Using Technology	3	Using computers to deliver teaching and learning resources
Technology in Technology	5.5	Publishing information on the Web
Technology in Technology	4.5	Video conferencing
Using Technology	1.1	Why change how we teach in higher education?
Using Technology	1.2	What are the options for change?

Figure 4.6   Essential differences between open and distance education

Open learning/education	Distance learning/education
Essentially on campus.	Essentially off campus at geographically different locations.
Very often mixed with traditional lectures and seminar teaching methods.	All teaching material is via a learning pack with a couple of weeks face to face.
Collaborative learning with peers possible and encouraged.	Essentially independent study but, with telecommunications, more collaborative work is possible in an electronic environment.
May need physical space and equipment to house open learning resources for student accessibility.	No extra space or equipment needed unless using telecommunications technology like computer conferencing, video conferencing and electronic mail or other Internet facilities such as World Wide Web. University overheads are in software and student support, rather than space and buildings.
Course tutors available locally for any trouble shooting or help.	Course tutors less easily available but with telecommunications via electronic mail, accessibility can increase (if tutors want this).
Need for policies to support students and integrate open teaching with more traditional methods.	Need for policies to support students. An increased use in technology will require more helpline services.
Open learning materials can rely on students being able to support their learning through the library.	Distance learning packages need to be all-inclusive as students may not have access to a library.
Open learning provides flexible access and encourages student independence. Electronic communication helps keep everyone in touch and sorts out problems quickly.	Distance learning provides the ultimate in flexible access and student independence. It can be isolating if electronic communication is not established.

Using Technology	4.4	Co-operative learning using computer conferencing
Using Technology	4.5	Managing electronic (virtual) groups
Using Technology	4.2	Communicating via email
Technology in Teaching	5	Using the World Wide Web
Using Technology	1.2	What are the options for change?

Open learning and distance learning are the most familiar terms we have in this field, but there are many more and all these 'alternative' methods have independent, collaborative or self-paced learning in common.

| Using Technology | 2 | Larger student groups: developing new teaching strategies |

Activity 4G   Is open/distance learning suitable for your course?

1 Is learning on your course best achieved at one time or place?

Yes ☐   No ☐

If 'yes', open and/or distance learning may not be an option for you. You can only consider electronic communication for course administration and self-help groups.

If you answered 'no', you are free to explore the open and/or distance learning options available to you. Explore your use of email, the WWW and computer conferencing if you have the chance. See if you can get your teaching and learning resources onto the network to increase access.
Are you familiar with writing open learning material?

2 Is tutor support required at set times?

Yes ☐   No ☐

If 'yes', open and/or distance learning may not be an option for you. Could you isolate why you need to be present and then find a solution that allows for collaborative learning among students?

If 'no', you can go ahead with open and/or distance learning. Encourage collaborative learning via electronic groups. You may also want to organize electronic sets to work on particular problems.